The Front Streets
of
Laramie City

by
Gladys B. Beery

Albany Seniors, Inc.
Laramie, Wyoming

The Front Streets of Laramie City

by Gladys B. Beery

Copyright 1990 by Gladys Beck Beery

Published by
Albany Seniors, Inc., a nonprofit corporation.
103 Ivinson Ave., Laramie, Wyoming.
Produced by Jelm Mountain Publications,
209 Park Street Laramie, Wyoming.

ISBN 0-936204-85-0

Cover photo: Laramie, Wyoming Territory, 1868. A town of shacks and tents. Note wandering paths and cluttered yards, and not a tree in town.

U.P. photo. Courtesy of Western History Research Center, University of Wyoming.

Acknowledgements

My sincere thanks to Rosa and LeRoy of Roman Photography; all personnel at the Western Research Center at the University of Wyoming; to Dr. T. A. Larson, Professor Emeritus of History, University of Wyoming, Mr. Emmett Chisum for his cheerful and interested help in Archival Department at the University of Wyoming; respected newspaperman, the late Ernest Linford; Agnes Burns for access to Dr. Robert Burns' book "Pioneer Ranches of Wyoming."

Special appreciation to Sandra E. Guzzo for translations of German language passages; to the Tuesday Night Writers for quality help and criticisms and "cheer-ups." To all persons who unknowingly gave tid-bits of information which added interest to this tale.

And most of all to my husband Lloyd for being a sounding-board.

A Special Note:

In recognition of one of Laramie's senior authors,
the publication of this book was sponsored by
Albany Seniors,
a nonprofit corporation that serves as caretaker for the
buildings at First and Ivinson
where the Senior Center is located.
Proceeds from the sale of this book will go to the
Laramie Aid to Seniors Trust
to help assure quality programs through the
Laramie Senior Center
in the years to come.

Foreword

Here is a word, and doubtless not the last, on the subject of Laramie City's early years, its bawd and building. It is as accurate a report as public records and newspaper reporting of the day (1870-1900). As there is no end to research, it is certain there is more than is related here.

Since the *Laramie Sentinel* is the only newspaper published in the new Territory which covers the entire thirty-year period included in this work, it is the principal source of reference. Granted, Hayford, the editor of the *Sentinel*, had his biases, but in the absence of other newssheets, his is the main and most consistent point of view. When other sources are available, they are included.

If J. H. Hayford seems to play a too-prominent role in the tale, it is justified. He, in a sense, molded Laramie City. If it failed to live up to his ideal as the Gem City of the Plains it was not for lack of trying on his part.

It may be noted that issues and problems that were dealt with on a day to day basis are little different from those confronted today and it is interesting to compare the ways these problems are met.

Sources

References supporting information contained in this book are principally; the *Daily and Weekly Sentinel,* since it is the one newssheet in publication covering the greater period cited in this manuscript, *The Laramie Republican*; *Laramie Republican-Boomerang,* and *Laramie Boomerang*; records at the Laramie Plains Museum and Albany County Public Library, the Western Heritage Research Center at the University of Wyoming and public records of Albany County Clerk, Clerk of Court, and the City of Laramie; *Laramie City Directory & History,* J. R. Triggs, 1875, *Laramie Daily Sentinel* printer, and *Trails of Yesterday,* by John Bratt, 1921, University of Nebraska Press.

Contents

Introduction

Where was Laramie's original front street, on the east or west side of the railroad tracks?

Where was the Big Tent pitched?

What was the normal use of the building in which the first woman jury met?

Where were the first five churches located?

When were the street names changed from the old ABC system?

Mrs. Gladys B. Beery authoritatively answers such questions and many more.

Gladys Beck was born on a farm in northeast Nebraska. As she was growing up she moved with her parents to Montana, northeastern Colorado, and back to central Nebraska, where she met and married Lloyd Beery in the little town of Farnam, Nebraska. The Beerys moved to Laramie in 1956.

In recent years Gladys has become recognized as the most knowledgeable authority on historic downtown buildings, and their owners, tenants, and uses, in the nineteenth century. For a number of years she worked in offices in the County Courthouse, where her work put her in touch with city and county records. After becoming acquainted with the variety of sources available in the Courthouse, and retiring from work there, she has devoted much of her spare time to gathering information from Courthouse records and from other sources outside the Courthouse. She has written articles, some of which have been published in the *Boomerang*. Much of her writing, however, is published for the first time in this book.

Gladys Beery's activity intersected with that of the Senior Center personnel several years ago. In working with the old buildings at First and Ivinson, and renovating them for use by the Senior Center, the board members of Albany Seniors, Inc. developed a deep interest in the early history of the neighborhood. They became so intrigued with downtown history that they decided to sponsor publication of this collection of Gladys Beery's stories.

With a unique style and frequent touches of humor Beery gives us insights into what sort of place the Gem City of the Plains really was in its youth. Sometimes she brings to mind the words of pioneer C. P. Arnold, prominent attorney, who in his old age more than 50 years ago protested "Don't talk to me about the noble pioneers. I knew some of the s.o.b.'s." Again, she makes us recall the philosopher Hobbes and the phrase he used to describe some of his antecedents, "nasty, brutish, and short."

Gladys seems to believe that females of all ages suffered more discrimination in the 19th Century in Laramie than they do now. She scoffs at the notion that the pioneer men in the West put women on a pedestal except in a few instances, and then publicly, not privately. In general, the many deprived, neglected, and abused women and children simply had no place to go for protection.

No question, Gladys dwells more on sinners than saints, perhaps unavoidably because there were so many sinners. Despite our current problems, Laramie is a much more civilized place than it was in the pioneer days. A few citizens, notably James H. Hayford, newspaper editor, and the Rev. J. A. Edmondson, Methodist minister, took up the cudgels for traditional Christian conduct, but it took considerable courage. She finds that even Hayford restrained himself when he found himself about to be overwhelmed.

Some leading pioneers are purposely rescued from obscurity. Their exploits, for one reason or another, have hitherto not been accorded the publicity given to some of their contemporaries. For example, the large Bath family, Henry and Charles Wagner, Patrick Doran, August and Charles Trabing, Michael H. Murphy, John and Lawrence Fee, John Bratt, Morgan Knadler, and George W. Fox.

Gladys includes tales about more brothels, saloons, breweries, dance halls, restaurants, and hotels and boarding houses than cities twice the size should have. She introduces us to many characters for the first time and gives life to what were merely names before.

Many writers have already contributed to Laramie lore. Gladys Beery is to be congratulated for supplying significant additions. I read the manuscript one night in one sitting and found it thoroughly enjoyable, even if somewhat shocking at times. I recommend it for the County Library's Wyoming Room and for everybody's "Know Your Laramie" shelf.

T. A. Larson — May 1, 1990

The Front Streets
of
Laramie City

One

There is only one Laramie.

There is a mountain range called Laramie, a peak called Laramie, two Laramie Rivers, "Big" and "Little" (the Little Laramie was once called Whiskey Creek), a wide, rolling upland basin known as the Laramie Plains, and a Fort Laramie, all in the state of Wyoming. But there is only one Laramie town.

A century ago someone remarked that "out west when two houses were built near each other it was called a town, and when a third was added it became a city."

When the Union Pacific Railroad reached the Laramie Plains of Dakota Territory in May of 1868, Laramie City was already there, a cluster of not three but 500 buildings. It was a fresh town smelling of raw planed lumber, new-cut logs, wet mud chinking and outdoor plumbing common to the day.

And this is the way it began:

In 1866 an unsightly collection of tents and shacks was huddled on Elizabeth (now Spring) Creek about two miles north of Fort Sanders, Dakota Territory. "Tin-town" was close to the river crossing of the Overland Stage Road and the emigrant road and so was there to serve travelers even before the railroad appeared on the Laramie Plains. Besides emigrants and knights of the road, there were the soldiers at the fort, always eager for relaxation and diversion from army monotony.

The surveyed railroad right-of-way for the Union Pacific line touched the west edges of this clutch of shanties. Dominating the camp was what later became known as the "Sunnyside" road house, a squalid place catering to thirsty soldiers, any weary traveler and those preoccupied with their pudenda.

When the survey of Laramie City was completed in October, 1867, a flurry of moving took place from the creek to the proposed townsite. A number of civilians attached to the fort made the move at the same time.

This new town could be just another railroad siding like so many which sprouted like weeds along the tracks and like weeds withered and died after the first flush of empire. Most of the regular track followers would stop only to skim top money from the camp then move on to next end-of-track town.

It wasn't important, then, the kind of building they occupied while acquiring their expected wealth, so many of the settlers set up tents, log-slab shacks, or upended ties or lodge-poles set into the ground and draped or covered them with canvas. Some merely planted four corner-posts in the ground and stretched cloth or canvas around or over. Many were the movable type, knocked down and moved from track's- end to track's-end. Some were fairly substantial with wood floors in the event they would remain for a long term. But most were dirt-floor, jerry-built shelters.

Lumber was to be had from anywhere in the mountains which girdled the high valley called the Laramie Plains. Tie cutters' camps and sawmills dotted the forested mountains between Cheyenne and the new town of Laramie City. Within months they had ravaged and nearly stripped the wooded hills.

One of the first business houses to rise on the site was Henry Wagner's dry goods tent-store, moved from Elizabeth Creek and placed in the centre of his squatter's tract. The land was not on sale until spring, but there were those early-comers who got the pick of sites, then bought when sales opened. Wagner also laid claim to what became known as Wagner's Private Alley.

The first hotel to appear at the proposed town-site was a long log building erected by Irish Patrick Doran and appropriately named the Shamrock, with flop-rooms at the back. Here the tall, lean boniface dispensed real Irish Cheer and the "best meals to be found, with rooms at reasonable rates."

Doran and four companions, all fresh from the "Old Sod," had arrived on the Laramie Plains in the early summer of 1867. M. H. Murphy, Doran, John and Lawrence Fee and John Connors had walked from the end-of-track at Pine Bluffs, Dakota Territory, bringing with them their worldly goods in a two-wheel cart. The Fees and Connors went to work at the Dawson Brothers' tie-camp up the Big Laramie River. Murphy got a job carrying chain for the survey gang which laid out Laramie City. Patrick saw other advantages and built his Shamrock where convivial men could gather 'round the flowing bowl and relax in good fellowship. Here too was to be had all the news and gossip that floated around the new country. The biggest advantage, of course, was a warm, sheltered place for the winter.

The Shamrock proved to be one of the immediate and biggest attractions in the new city on the plains, particularly so when Pat's unique bookkeeping system became known. Doran kept his accounts posted on a blacked board on the back wall. When the bill was paid, Doran erased it from the board. Each customer's bill was plainly writ where all could see. Perhaps the first to object was one deep in his cups, and easy-going Patrick wiped it from the board to avoid argument. But it soon became known that if someone claimed that the bill was not correct, the Irishman wiped the slate clean, and over the years this trick was too often used. Doran went broke, lost his saloon to mortgage and unpaid taxes, lost his homestead and livestock and wound up in the County Poor Farm which stood on part of his former homestead. He died a pauper, loved, but laughed at, an easy-going fool.

The new settlement on the Laramie Plains really burst into full life a few months before the arrival of the Union Pacific railroad. When the first lots were sold in April, 1868, there were already more than 500 buildings strung out near the Big Laramie River where the land drained gently toward the stream.

While those early birds settled on the newly platted town site, the Union Pacific was stalled in Cheyenne for the winter of 1867. It proved to be a rough one, but in May the tracks were laid over the hills into the great, splendid valley of the Laramie Plains. And when the first train puffed its way into town with bell ringing, whistle screaming, steam gushing, smoke belching in black clouds from the great stack, the town was there.

The string of flatcars was loaded with goods and laughing shouting passengers. They yelled, waved, discharged their guns toward the keen blue sky, and the town was there, waiting for them all.

The *Frontier Index*, that famous "saucy" newspaper on wheels, which had been created at Fort Kearney, Nebraska Territory, and paced the rails westward, was already in town. The Freeman brothers, Virginians, lately become galvanized Yanks, could have remained in quarters at Fort Sanders except for Brother Legh's spicy, uncalled for remarks about General Gibbon's southern background. For this "sauce" the good general expelled the brothers from the fort with their wagons, press and worldly goods.

No matter, the whole basin was empty, the horizons were broad. And waiting.

The pair drove to the new town site and hired A. S. Blackburn to build for them a house. It was a log structure, big enough to house all their newspaper accoutrements with living room for themselves, and extra rooms to let. They rented the extra rooms to L. B.

Wright, named the building the "Frontier Hotel" after their *Index*, and settled down to work.

The Frontier Hotel in time touched the edges of fame when a shed on the back lot served as gallows for the first hoodlum to be hung in the initial effort to clean up the town.

Later the famous black bronc-buster known as Bronco Sam (Stewart) lived in the hotel with his Indian wife, Kitty, and it was here that Sam (who "did not drink to excess") shot and killed her for supposed infidelity as reported to him by "friends." He then turned the gun on himself and staggered, bleeding, into the street intersection of Second and South C (Garfield). Friends picked him up and took him to the hospital where he died a few days later.

It was here, too, that William Crout, Proprietor, caught one of his customers and "trounced him good" for committing a nuisance on the floor of the lobby after too prolonged acquaintance with Crout's sample room. The customer was much too relaxed to suffer grievous injury except to dignity, and Crout cheerfully paid the fine for assault and welcomed the customer back to the brass-rail.

It was in the back yard of the Frontier that Crout, himself, a year later, was shot for making unkind and ungentlemanly remarks about a woman rooming there. There was some legal activity over that, and a bit of gun-play, but the woman went home to her husband in Cheyenne and Crout recovered, although he noticeably favored one side when he sat down.

The *Frontier Index* moved on in the fall of 1868 to follow the excitement of the railroad westward, and met its fate at Bear River City on the west side of the Rocky Mountains.

To supply ties to the railroad and building and heating materials for all the new settlers and businesses took many hands. The activity in the Laramie mountain range (called the Black Hills at that time) and the surrounding hills kept the valley echoes ringing. And if the noise of axe-men and screaming sawmills and the following noises of trains wasn't enough, the rest was supplied by life in the village sprawling on the banks of the Laramie River.

One tie-camp alone hired six hundred woodsmen. With men from twenty or so other woodcamps in the area plus soldiers from Fort Sanders, all seeking diversion, the town pulse was always beating pretty fast.

The six-hundred-man camp operated by Gilman-Carter (later Coe-Carter) was located two and a half miles northeast of the fort and known as the Fort Sanders woodcamp.

There was no connection between the military establishment and the woodcamp except perhaps the rancor aroused when tee- totaler John Bratt, who was storekeeper and paymaster for the company, hauled the camp's entire liquor supply over to the fort and sold it to Alexander Steele, post sutler.

Bratt stood up to the angry tie-hacks and told them they could leave any time they weren't satisfied. Having liquor in camp stirred up too many fights and other troubles. Since this company paid and fed better and more promptly than most of the other camps, only a few men left.

The outdoor work in all kinds of weather, Bratt agreed, made it desirable to ward off damp, chills and fevers and so the men kept liquor around for "medicinal purposes." But it was not sold in camp.

It took a sizeable amount of spirits to keep a lumber camp or sawmill operating, so the supply frequently ran low, but more could be obtained from the sutler or in Laramie City, and the crews always welcomed change, and that too could be found in town. Sometimes it also took sizeable doses of spirits to loosen the aching joints of timbermen, so by the time they were properly relaxed, the town itself had a glow on and very often the medicine taken in the Front Street dives brought on peculiar side-effects that were only cured by fists, knives or guns.

Every frontier town had its Front Street teeming with life, some livelier and/or more important than others. But Laramie City was different. It had two.

The original Front Street paralleled the Union Pacific railroad tracks and lay between the rail yards and Big Laramie River. The high water table and swampy bottomland was not ideal for heavy building. Add to that the tie-drives that rode the high waters in springtime, and the fact that when the tracks were being laid snow was melting in the high mountains west and south and river water sloshed too close to the laid tracks, so it was clear that the banks of the stream should not hold too many parcels of the town.

So the east side of the tracks was the preferred side. It was higher and drained well. Most popular and first settled were the three streets immediately east of the rail yards. Although legally designated as First Street, the one at track side became known as "Front Street," and included second and third streets almost as a unit.

Before long the original Front Street became a dim shadow of its wilder twin and some years later when the town got around to giving the streets names rather than letters, it was re- named Pine Street. There was never any envy of the east Front.

The town's business section stretched from South D (Custer) north to Centre (University) Street. Around, between and among the sinful establishments were small houses and cabins where lived the more sedate townspeople. Most shopkeepers followed the old tradition of living in rooms at the back of their business, or in flats upstairs. This proximity to the heady sounds of night life must have been rough on the sleep and rest of the more stable citizens, particularly since there was no such thing as sound-proofing in those days.

Life in Laramie City was so fast and dangerous that even the toughs walked wide and easy, and it was only prudent for a man to walk down the middle of the street, even in broad daylight. The saying was true: "Ya'd better walk soft if ya wanta walk long in the west."

One of the main entertainment centres, during that first summer, and perhaps the randiest of the lot, was the Big Tent.

The Big Tent was a huge structure covering two city lots, each 24 feet wide, and reaching from the alley on South A (Thornburgh/Ivinson) to Second Street. Actual size as given by Will Owen is 50 feet by 132. It was "canvas stretched over scantling frame, with wooden floor," and stood on South A Street where the "Midwest Block" building (formerly Kassis now the Jean Junction), now stands covering approximately the same space.

Will Owen, who later worked with a survey team to map the whole of Wyoming, was a boy of nine or ten in 1868. In his unpublished memoirs (Roach Collection at the Laramie Plains Museum) Owen tells of Laramie's early days. His recollection of the Big Tent is told in part:

> . . . the Big Tent . . . had every gambling device and game known to the fraternity. It stood just across the street from our house . . . I mention this joint in particular because immediately in front of it occurred the first murder I ever witnessed. Not only were gambling games to be found there . . . it was a hurdy-gurdy of the vilest sort. All day and night without cessation dancing was in full swing, the women portion of the dancers being the lowest of the low, . . . camp followers who had followed the railway from its inception. There were probably twenty-thirty of these women in that Big Tent, and it was their business to dance with any man who asked them and lead him to the bar for refreshment. Drinks were 25 cents each and dances very

short . . . Night and day we could hear the calls: 'Alla-
mande left'; 'Balance all'; 'Grand right and left'; 'Swing
your partners' and 'Promenade to the Bar.' At frequent
intervals came the strident announcement of the Keno
dealer: 'And Keno is Kee- rect!'

. . . the wild revelry never ended. Shooting and stabbing
affairs in that Hell Hole were frequent. One day in the
summer of 1868 I was sitting by our front window . . . (and
saw) . . . a rush of men and women from the Tent. They
came out in wild disorder, scattering in every direction . . .
Out of this crowd ran two men directly toward our house,
one of them with a pistol in his hand. The first man had
reached the middle of the street when his pursuer fired the
revolver and dropped him in his tracks. A crowd gathered
around the fallen figure . . . a few minutes later the victim
was carried to a room upstairs in the building that years
afterward became known as 'Jackrabbit Johnson's
Place' . . . .

Owen stated that the man survived only a few
minutes. The people "seemed more interested in the
bullet-riddled sign board near our house than in the
man." And within ten minutes after the shots were fired
the excitement had subsided, the street was clear, the
games going full blast and the cry "Promenade to the
Bar" again filling the air. No arrests were made, hardly
any comment was uttered. Everything went on as if
nothing unusual had happened.

Nothing unusual had happened. Such incidents
were a regular thing. With the rounds of business in the
half-light houses and bottle-men thick in grogshops and
sample rooms of the various hotels, such occurrences
were frequent.

Thomas Robinson's saloon on South A had nightly
battles, sometimes ending with shooting or stabbing.
More often arguments were settled by razor in that dark
man's log shack.

Tom Fagen could boast a few broken heads day or
night in his Second Street oasis which he called the

Alhambra, standing next to the first Spanish Bazaar, a store owned by the Sutphen Brothers. They later built the first stone structure in town over on South A, just west of the former location of the Big Tent. But that was after the grand Exodus.

Over on the other side of the block, on First Street, stood the fabled "Diana," unabashedly advertised in the *Frontier Index* as the "largest sporting house west of New York." The irony is inescapable for Diana, goddess of the hunt, was also goddess of chastity and marriage.

The real name of the place was Crisman's House. It was a large building located on the southwest corner of the lot at First and South B (Grand). Several ratty buildings or shacks stood on the back of the lots. Next to the back door of Diana stood a tent-dance hall and clear back on the alley stood the popular Tivoli.

Established by a tall, thin-necked fellow named Jay C. Crisman (Chrisman) in the first days of Laramie, his Diana, besides its early notoriety, stayed in operation until 1896 under numerous names.

Crisman first sold the place to Valentine Baker, who also ran Childs' House two blocks south. Baker changed the Diana to the "European Hotel," partly to erase the stigma lingering from Crisman days, and to establish the place as a respectable family hotel with a sense of sophistication, something the residents of any frontier town seemed to feel necessary.

Custom in Laramie seemed to vary so much that a proprietor could stay in business only for a short time, and Baker soon sub-let the place, first to Andy Erisman, (Sheriff) then to Halstead and Apperson, "eminent hotel-men." The name "European" was retained by both lessors and advertised as "The Favorite House in the West."

Business flourished but Baker didn't pay and Crisman was obliged to repossess the property. Then he sold to Colonel Noah Worth who remodeled the original building and added space for his store. Crisman moved out to his horse ranch east of town. A few years later he was shot in the head by the two young men he had hired to help drive a horse herd to market. They, of course, were caught, tried and sent to prison for eighteen months, more for horse-stealing than the murder. And no one remembered that Jay C. Crisman, keeper of a house of prostitution, had also served as a member of that first city government which lasted only three weeks.

Colonel Worth, who bought the old hotel/brothel, did some handsome remodeling and opened his business with added dry goods and groceries lining the walls of the lobby. His devotion to the chess-board led to the first serve-yourself store in the Territory of Wyoming. Any customer was told to find what he wanted. It was a job to pry Worth from his game to wrap and accept payment for the goods.

The Worth name remained above the door for many years and then a member of the Bath family took over the place.

One of the Bath descendants, in writing about the family, remarked that the first Baths on the Plains apparently felt it their duty to populate the county all by themselves. There were enough Baths to operate every hotel and saloon in town, and at one time or another they did.

When Theodore Bath took over the old Worth Hotel he refurbished and renamed it the "Laramie Hotel." When that burned down in 1896 another hotel was built on the same corner and named for the owner: the Johnson Hotel, which still stands.

Of much more interest is the Tivoli, another watering hole recorded in every early history of Laramie City. This particular oasis was one of the most popular in town and it stood on the alley at the east end of the "Diana" lots.

Built in 1868 by Crisman, later sold to freighter

'Pap' Rice and his wife Euphemia (Emia), the old Tivoli Hall became the "Centennial" in 1876 under proprietorship of Henry Goetz and Henry Bath. They worked the place over and added a second story with hotel accommodation. In one of these rooms in the Centennial one Ben Murphy, a banjo player at the Variety Theatre, gained temporary fame by being found in his bed with a bullet in a vital area. It was said that his real name was Merrill B. Hoyt, and his "sensitive nature" had been so deeply wounded by his wife's desertion that he took up a life of dissipation and "died as the fool dieth."

Then Peter Holt leased the Centennial. Holt, an Englishman, was pleased to style himself as "supplier to Her Majesty the Queen, President Grant" and others of note. He arrived in Laramie in 1869 and set about operating a fruit and vegetable store with confectionery on First Street between Center and South A. During his early prosperity he built an elaborate Victorian Gothic house for his wife Florette, who had left him two months after their marriage in 1866 in Steadmanville, New York. Florette never returned to Holt and in 1875 he finally obtained a divorce. The house still stands on South Tenth Street in Laramie, a lovely monument to Peter's unrequited love.

Holt lost the Front Street store, five lots of land and his elegant home. Now, in the old Tivoli-Centennial in 1877, he, too, had had some remodeling done, perhaps the better to serve the Queen and President Grant. John H. Davis had done the work for which he hadn't received full payment, so Davis called on Holt.

Embarrassed and angered at being publicly dunned, the Queen's supplier went after the carpenter with a butcher knife. Davis escaped but not before the back of his coat suffered. A customer in the saloon/hotel stopped Holt with a poker applied to his head. Holt, the customer told the Sheriff, "was ravin' drunk."

Another Tivoli owner, in later years, was a wife-beater who spent time (off and on) in the town calaboose. His wife eventually came into ownership of the bar-room and years later died of excessive use of alcoholic beverages.

In 1893 she had sold the historic old watering hole to John Huempfner, Laramie's "Beer King." The King tore down the old landmark that had supplied Her Majesty for a time, and hired George Berner to build in its place the structure standing today at 111 Grand.

Until 1870 there were only four or five hotels in the village. Over on West Front were Wilcox's hotel and livery and another whose name is lost in the mists of time; on the east side were the Frontier, Doran's Shamrock, Crisman's House (appealing to its select clientele) and Childs, a genuine family-style hotel.

Childs never made the newspapers, other than in small box- ads, nor did it even make the grapevine, and it soon disappeared. It stood on the corner at Front and South C (Garfield). The site later served as a railroad park and is now a parking lot.

Then there was the first railroad hotel. It was combination freight-house-hotel and ticket-office, and stood on the main line in the yards near South B.

When the Union Pacific Company found need for a reliable and steady supply of water for their hotel, they hired men to dig a well near the building. And it was then that a flush of gold fever hit Laramie City.

John Bratt and friend Gilman happened into town from their woodcamp over east and stopped by to watch the shovelmen. The well had reached a depth close to twenty feet when the men quit for dinner. While they were gone Gilman decided to make their work more interesting. He had a small poke of gold which he sprinkled into the well. There was enough water in the bottom to allow much of the gold to sink, but it was quickly detected once the workmen began digging again. The cry "GOLD! GOLD!" went up, the digging stopped and a horde of men swarmed onto the site, pushing, shoving, cursing and fighting to stake claims as close to "Discovery" as they could. Many black eyes, cuts, bruises and sore heads later, and with one man dead, Gilman decided the joke had gone for enough and confessed the hoax. Only a lot of loud, fast talk, many cigars and drinks and the price of a coffin were all that saved him from joining the deceased.

The cuts and broken heads were patched up by Dr. John Finfrock at the railroad's tent hospital up in the 100 block on Second Street. The dead man was interred in the first city cemetery away out east of town, seven blocks from the business section. And the incident was forgotten by the town.

Two

It is accepted that the dregs of society followed the rails. So, too, did honest men. Surveyors, railroad grading crews, tie-cutters, track men (those famed Gandy-dancers, so called for the tools they used which were manufactured by the Gandy Tool Company of Chicago), freighters, merchants — they all lived off the railroad money.

This great westward movement brought from the east many doubtful characters. The tough ones, the crooks, the crude and rude opened trails and wherever they trod, so 'tis said, "there went the Jug of Empire," and civilization followed.

Here on the enormous Laramie Plain, framed on all sides by lifting, silent mountains and stretching to the indefinite northward horizon, here beneath a splendid, cloudless sky, people could behave as themselves without legal restrictions or psychiatry. And they did. Inhibitions were forgotten and the lawless ruled. For a time. That time was reached in Laramie City in August of 1868 when the foundling city was barely three months old.

Asa Moore (Ace Moyer) and his gang had run roughshod over the town and countryside during that time and too many honest men had wound up in Moore's back room, robbed and dead, later to be hauled out of town and callously dumped into some ravine.

So the "decent" men gathered secretly in a back room of Pap Rice's Tivoli and hatched their scheme to rid the town of undesirables.

A quick foray by the first "vigilance committee" ended in the hanging of a minor thug called The Kid in a shed behind the Frontier Hotel. This only slowed some of the activities, but really changed nothing. The big chiefs of the riff-raff continued as they were. The first attempt at city government, undertaken in the early days of the town, was a failure. All officials resigned after three weeks in office. The gamblers and grafters appointed themselves to office and had things under their control.

In October another vigilante group was organized. This time plans were better laid and more complete. They were to make a clean sweep of town and it could have worked but some hot-head became nervous or too anxious for glory (or perhaps it was a sympathizer wanting to warn "the element') and fired his gun before the official signal was given. The result was a quick, furious battle and the gamblers' luck ended with the capture and hanging of three ringleaders of the gang, Asa Moore, Con Wager and Big Ed Wilson.

The committee passed word to the rest of the high-rollers that their health would be better found elsewhere. So brisk was the exodus that it was said they never even left footprints.

Morning found a quieter town, but there were a few hangers-on, who thought they could get by. This was remedied by introducing one "Big Steve" or "Long Steve" Young to a rope and telegraph pole near the railroad freight depot. The others were convinced and shook off the dust of Laramie, so for a time the little town enjoyed a breathing spell.

By fall the *Frontier Index*, too had moved on to meet its fate at the hands of a mob in Bear River City on the other side of the Rocky Mountains. The *Index* perished but Legh Freeman survived to chronicle other tales of other towns.

The purging of the village wasn't a genuine house cleaning but it was a good dust-job. Many of the dives and gaming joints and houses of ill-repute continued as before. The difference now was that the proprietors were "old settlers along the border." The rough-handers were gone and it depended now on who owned certain properties where "unseemly conduct" was conducted whether items were published in the town's newspaper or over village bars and teacups.

It was onto this scene, early in the spring of 1869 after the *Index* had gone, that James H. Hayford and J. E. Gates appeared. They were operating a newspaper owned by N. A. Baker of Cheyenne and they called it the *Laramie Sentinel.* By May 1, 1870, the pair had purchased the plant from Baker and it became the voice of the Plains and Laramie. It was in this news sheet that the publicity was accomplished — or hushed up.

The *Sentinel* was first located on the second floor of A. T. Williams' Bakery on Laramie's tough Front Street, so was in the thickest of the Street's activities. Hayford gathered his own news and did most of the hand work. He, like all early editors, freely expressed his personal opinions on all subjects, often as news items. Hayford and Gates were partners, but the paper was Hayford's tool.

Like Legh Freeman, he loved the beautiful, wild Laramie valley and adopted the theme that Laramie City was The Gem of the Plains and would become an important point on the Union Pacific line.

Hayford promoted the town in language sometimes bordering on ecstatic and carefully shielded its pure name. He did, though, allow his angers, biases and favoritisms to appear in his paper, but certain personalities were often spared. Others were given the well-honed edge of his metaphors and one of these was Charles Bramel, one of Laramie's able attorneys.

Bramel was from Missouri and just as wordy and opinion-proud as the newspaperman. At one time Bramel published his own newspaper so that he could publicly express his opinions on the same footing and with as wide an audience. His sheet, the Chronicle, lived less than two years and put him in frequent verbal exchange with Hayford and led to his oft-quoted remark that Hayford could "throw more mud with a teaspoon than I can with a scoop shovel."

Hayford depended on no one for his impressions, often poked fun at pomposity, was a bit pompous himself openly admired the ladies and had strong opinions about where they belonged. Just as strong were his ideas on bringing up the family. He is said to have fathered twenty-one children, according to W. E. Chaplin, a contemporary newspaperman.

Hayford had a keen wit and the columns of the *Sentinel* were well dusted with his humor before the advent of Edgar Wilson (Bill) Nye who seemed to have made many other humorists of the day seem dull.

Hayford neither drank nor swore, although he did once declare a newsman's frustrations and aggravations were enough to drive him to it. He did, however, chew 'baccy, and friends and acquaintances alike poked fun at his habit.

When the weather was cold enough to stop the flies, it was said, Hayford stashed his chew outside the church door where it would keep until the service was over and he could again attach it to his jaw.

He seemed to enjoy attending meetings and riling the ladies by aiming in the general direction of the spittoon. At each time the spittoon would be moved to his target area only to have him aim at another spot.

James Hayford became an important part of the early days of Laramie City and faithfully worked for her betterment. It might even be said that he molded the city himself, smoothing over her wrinkles and hiding her blemishes and those of his friends while blatantly trumpeting the shortcomings of foes. Sometimes in fits of pique he even exposed some lack in his friends, but that was quickly countered by reporting a few of their finer points.

Hayford has been called "goody-goody" for his moral and religious convictions. He frowned heavily on those who followed the wide and wandering path, but he didn't always call a spade a spade. There were many places where he gave light lip-service when his full voice might have changed events.

He was a busy man who aired his views, which were many, on any and all subjects, and demonstrated that he, unlike the boy who could not ride his bicycle and chew gum at the same time, could live his full, rich and busy life and chew tobacco at the same time.

In those first months buildings were thrown together quickly with little or no regard for appearance. When later this lack of aesthetics was corrected and better, more handsome structures were raised — on borrowed money, or on "time" for the workmen, unsettled accounts drew interest after thirty days from date of the last-sold item. Thus mechanics' liens were filed immediately, for even though a handshake could seal a bargain it didn't pay the bill and there was need for legal proof of money due. The records of liens are accurate, are of public record, and an invaluable help in tracing a town's history.

Wood was the principal building material, but as soon as a decent brick could be turned out, "soft" though it was, it was more frequently used.

Brick was made at three different yards on the banks of the Big Laramie River where proper soil could be found, with plenty of water at hand. A slaughterhouse was convenient, also, if animal hair and blood were wanted for binder.

The earliest brick turned out sold at 2 ¢ each, later

the price was ½ ¢ "delivered to the wall," and the yards were kept busy. Even so, there were bankruptcies. There is no evidence that the product turned out by convict labor after the Territorial Prison was built in 1872 could be had any cheaper than at a private yard.

Building rock of excellent quality was also available not far from the little town, and could replace brick at less cost, but lack of good stone cutters at the quarries and good masons to lay up the stone was another inducement to using brick. Uncut rock was used in basement foundation walls with dirt and cement as filler.

A quarry where Peacock-stone was cut operated for a time under the management of Al Cook and A. P. Smith. The stone, of remarkable beauty, was deep pink in color and may be seen in a few of the stone houses in Laramie.

Most of the stone from area quarries is a lighter cream with darker lacings. The enduring quality and grace of the early buildings at the University of Wyoming demonstrates the powerful beauty of stone-craft.

However, those first years saw only frame and log buildings, and with such a warren of them, and the use of wood for heat, and with coal-oil for lighting, it is a miracle there were so few fires. Perhaps because everyone was acutely aware of the hazard particular care was taken.

Early organization and the efficiency of volunteer fire fighters kept fire to a minimum. When one did occur the hosemen were quickly on the spot so losses were kept low.

When one of Ludolph Abrams little wood huts, occupied by Dr. Voerpooten as Drugstore and office, caught fire, the hoseboys couldn't save it, but they did manage to keep it from the frame New York House only feet away to the south and from John Fischer's Saloon and Reading Rooms on the corner of the block now occupied by the Overland Deli.

One of the hose-chasers was, of course, Editor Hayford. Like today's news media, it was his right to run and report and the people's right to know. Since the *Sentinel* was housed on Front Street, they were in the vanguard of most of the action. Later, when they could afford it, the company built a two-story brick block on the east side of Second Street just south of the City Hall with its booming fire-bell. The newspaper operation was on the second floor of their new building and on a level with the bell tower so it's no wonder Hayford complained about the volume of the bell. "Loud enough to be heard five miles out of town. A real boomer!" he termed it. And in those days there was nothing to stop the echo from the Black Hills to Sheep Mountain forty miles away.

South of the *Sentinel* building stood the long log structure once occupied by Edward A. Ivinson as a grocery-and-provision store. The building had been used for a short time as a drugstore by N. K. Boswell before he became the first Warden at the Territorial Penitentiary and later took up the more rigorous and exciting life of law enforcement.

Ivinson bought the building and ran a modest grocery business from it. In his City Directory for 1875, J. H. Triggs described Ivinson as a "Capitalist." Many people perceived the man differently, from just plain lucky to an astute business man to outright crook. Upon occasion Hayford, when in a pettish mood, referred to him as "Evergreen Ivinson." Whatever anyone thought of the man, all agreed that he was ambitious, a good worker and not too proud to personally deliver groceries in his own wheelbarrow. Ivinson certainly valued himself. He never gave up his seat at table, which may have irritated a number of people, for he always "sat above the salt."

Edward Ivinson sold his store in 1872 to Clark and Heinrod and bought the bank that had been started in

Laramie City by H. J. Rogers and Posey Wilson of Cheyenne and Denver. Later he built his own brick block, a two-story affair with imposing iron front.

The bank occupied part of the main floor and the Ivinsons lived in a flat on the second floor until around 1890. A portion of the second floor was used as party room, theatre and dance hall and general meeting place for public functions and naturally was called "Ivinson Hall."

In later years, after the A. S. Peabody grocery store was gone and before the present Woolworth Company took over the building, some entrepreneur set up a small liquor still and began "rectifying" his own booze in an unused closet on the second floor. The operation was discovered and reported to authorities who came and dismantled the works and heartlessly dumped about 15 gallons of mash.

꧁ঌ৺꧂

There were small grocery and provision businesses catering to the public before the town grew to proportions that could support big dealers. These were to be found in small dark places where rent was cheap and space not overwhelming. Some of them were located in those shops so hurriedly vacated in the exodus of '68.

Marsh and Cooper ran their Pacific Meat Market on Second Street; Hutton's People's Market was a popular place to trade and over on South B (Grand) across the alley from the Tivoli was where Mike Quann had his grocery.

Quann was a popular figure about town, and upon his return from the venture with George Fox in the Black Hills of Dakota, he had opened his grocery business in partnership with brother John. It, too, was a good-going business when Mike Quann died at age 33, highly esteemed and mourned by his peers. Quann was a drunkard and died "an unfortunate victim of a bad habit."

"Quann's" remained a fixture in the town's business world for years, under management of brother John who had inherited the business, and unfortunately a taste for the bottle as well. He died in 1894 of acute alcoholism. He left no relatives and ownership of the store passed to John Blair, a long-time employee.

Another business which became a big operation during one of the boom periods of Laramie was that of James Bannon and Philip Mandell who put up their brick grocery store at the corner of Second and South C, opposite Trabing's and Holliday's.

These three stores, all built within two years' time, formed a formidable triangle of competition. Bannon and Company later evolved into the Co-Operative Grocery, and later still became the Laramie Grocery Company.

The regular stores were subject to irregular fluctuations of other markets just as now. In many ways they were more vulnerable because their prosperity depended on whether or not ranchers, farmers and other rural people were successful in getting pay for their season's labors. The rural hired help, also, depended totally on seasonal pay, thus businessmen in town must borrow operating money while extending credit to their customers. If prices were low for farmer or rancher, business in town suffered as well as the rural areas. So bankruptcies, although considered the depths of disgrace, were not isolated incidents.

There were several big operators in the merchandising game at one time or another in Laramie. The earliest merchants were small-scale venturers and many lost their shirts after the railroad money slowed down.

One of the busier suppliers from the very beginning of Laramie City was that first merchant, Henry Wagner. With his brother Charles, they conducted their stores in

Laramie and Cheyenne plus a freight line of sizeable proportions. Their heaviest freighting operations were west and southwest up the North Platte River Valley, and over into the Meeker and White River Agency area of Colorado. They ran a line north out of Fort Steele and up to the Indian Territory of the Shoshone and Crow. Their combination was so successful that they had erected one of the finest of the first brick buildings in Laramie. The wide scope of their business seemed to warrant a large building, but they were a modest pair and settled for modest quarters in a two-story building 24 feet by 66 feet with "plate glass front," the first in town.

Henry was elected as one of the first County Commissioners but for unstated reasons failed to attend meetings. He neither responded to letters of inquiry, nor to demands to appear, nor did he answer when threatened with fines for non-performance of civic duties.

No explanation for his absence is given in the Commissiosner's Proceedings, but a Certificate of Doctor of Medicine, issued at Bellevue Hospital in New York, is recorded in Albany County Records. The date covers the period of his absence from the Commissioners' meetings, and may provide the explanation.

There is no evidence, however, that Henry ever practiced medicine around Laramie or Albany County. It could be that he felt a need of medical knowledge for caring for his family. An infant son had died just before the Bellevue studies. The knowledge could have been useful, too, for their freighters, exposed to all the hazards of the trail.

The brothers eventually went bankrupt and moved with their respective families to Colorado. The Trabing Brothers Mercantile Company successfully filled the gap left by Wagners.

August Trabing's first business in Laramie was as

grog-seller in a 40-foot long frame-over-log building just south of Patrick Doran's Shamrock Hotel on First Street. The front of the shop had been painted a rather violent blue which served for a half-century to identify the place. The official name was "The National Theatre," but it was known by everyone as the "Old Blue Front," and here, in addition to the liquid dispensed over the bar, was offered vaudeville entertainment, usually for men only, which added to its attraction.

An article appearing in the *Laramie Daily Boomerang's* Centennial Jubilee issue (1868-1968) states:

> "The history of the building as recounted by early day residents, was most colorful. It reportedly had served as den for three desperadoes who were later hanged. It was also used as a theatre for the traveling groups that used to arrive via the U. P. Railroad to brighten the city's night life."

According to all Laramie history, the only three desperadoes hanged during the period referred to were the Moore-Wagner-Wilson trio. Other hangings were one-man affairs. If this reminiscence is correct, then the Old Blue Front was also the infamous "Bucket of Blood."

The location of the National Theatre, which may have got its name from the Trabings, was near the corner of Front and South C (First and Garfield), and quite handy to the John Keane cabin two blocks away where the men were strung up.

Pictures of Laramie City in 1868 show trails and paths wandering, directionless, across lots and any seriously inspired vigilantes wouldn't want to go far to conduct a hanging. Since there was not a tree in town for several more years, the best place for this type justice was the summer beam of an unfinished cabin. And Keane's was handy.

August Trabing's first wife, Ulrike Zastrow, had bought the grogshop in July, 1869 a year after the pair arrived in Laramie City. She had apparently operated the place herself earlier in the year before buying the buildings from Paul Fuhr, who had served as houseman for Ed Shaunessey who had moved into the joint after the hangings of the Moore gang.

Mrs. Trabing had some assistance from her husband who was fulfilling a tie-and-wood contract at Lookout, a siding on the railroad about 20 miles west of Laramie. Young 'Gus, already portly with the belly often referred to as a German goiter, liked to relate in later years how he had kept the National Theatre in operation by frequently appearing on the stage there. He did attain "star billing" a quarter century later as a singing comedian in Laramie's famous Maennorchor, a group of singer-actors of German extraction.

The National Theatre caused the Trabings to be indicted for "keeping a theatre without paying Special Tax" to the United States government. They were fined $25. Also on the same date August Trabing plead not guilty to "Retailing Liquors without paying Special Tax." This also was instituted by the Government. This suit was dismissed.

By December, 1869, August Trabing had obtained substantial contracts with the government for hauling their freight and supplies to Fort Fetterman on the North Platte River and on into the far northern wilderness of Wyoming Territory and the southern reaches of Montana along the beautiful Yellowstone River Valley. There seemed hardly a place where this hard-headed German businessman did not venture with his huge freight wagons.

These freighting enterprises made a move necessary. The railroad hauled the government goods to a depot at Medicine Bow, 60 miles west on the U.P. line. So August and eighteen-year-old Ulrike Trabing moved to the Medicine Bow station, an old stage stop on the military road between Forts Laramie, Fetterman and

Steele, and later made famous by Owen Wister's cowboy tale "The Virginian."

Ulrike leased her saloon on Front Street to Charles Kuster, one of the numerous German residents of Laramie City, and went with August to Medicine bow. When younger brother Charles arrived in Wyoming, the brothers remodeled the blue-painted National Theatre in Laramie and opened it as a small store and storage warehouse. Operated in conjunction with the Medicine Bow business, it became known as Trabing's Blue Front and the logo was carried on their advertising and stationery for many years.

As with the brothers, business successes followed and the Trabings added more warehousing space to the Blue Front and expanded all operations, which included logging and mining. One of the regular log drives brought 78,000 ties down the Big Laramie River. Others ran in similar amounts. But this was apparently not usual, for Trabing's did things in a big way, always.

Their venture into gold and copper mining in the area added to their fortunes, and a new freight-line south to Cummins City near the Wyoming-Colorado border and on to the Walden-North Park area and Hahn's Peak Mining District in northern Colorado made storage an added necessity. Trabing's 36-team trains were a common sight along all freighting trails of early-day Wyoming.

Their business grew as did their ambitions. They helped organize Savings and Loan companies in Laramie, the town's Board of Trade and several business corporations of repute on which their names appeared as officers and trustees.

By 1883 the brothers owned the entire south half of the block on Garfield (South C) between First and Second Streets and had built a gigantic emporium that would put any 20th century business west of the Mississippi to shame.

They may not in the beginning, have had plans for so big an establishment, but Morgan Knadler and Charlie Rand were set on erecting their new livery stable on the lots adjoining the great store on the north, and that could not be tolerated. So the Trabings acquired those two lots, first by lease, later by purchase, and added a second 48-foot by 132-foot section to their already huge building.

They celebrated the completion of the new building with a Grand Pretzel Ball.

The company received raves in publicity in the home papers. Hayford reminded all and sundry of their "ignominious beginnings as grogsellers on First Street." Newspapers in other towns joined in the chorus of praise. The raves were justified.

Fine offices were panelled in high-grade walnut, gas lighting was used throughout the building and included handsome street-lighting along Garfield and in front of the emporium. (Gas had been lately introduced into Laramie, so this alone lent glamor to the edifice.)

Great stacks of merchandise lined all walls and rose ceiling high in the warehouses. Plush family quarters were installed on the second floor of the store, although August had a fine new Italianate style home on South B (Grand) Street. The whole lay-out was heated by a fine modern furnace.

This heating system caused the disastrous fire which destroyed the Trabing Mercantile empire in 1895. Unfortunately, brother Charles had died tragically ten years earlier when he contracted blood-poisoning from a seemingly harmless scratch on his hand. So the vast business had been carried on by August. The ambition and drive were his, as was the loss.

After the terrible conflagration, the company opened another store and continued in business on a lesser scale, but never did recover from that disastrous financial blow. Trabing died with assets much below

$8,000 after having reached wealth close to the million dollar range.

᠅᠅᠅᠅᠅

The other and main business rival to Trabing was the W. H. Holliday Company which followed the same rise and fall route — start small, grow, expand, build and build until it, too, suffered the same fate as Trabing.

When William Crout decided to quit the Laramie Scene he sold the quarter block occupied by the historic Frontier Hotel "with messuage."* Crout had added a large three-story frame building to the west, facing on Second Street and attached to the original log structure. Holliday's first store section reared itself within feet of the Frontier Hotel, another aggravation to Crout. Crout had had enough trouble with that property. In 1883, while the Hotel and bar were leased to James Brown, tragedy struck.

Pinepoles had been laid over an old well on the north side of the building, and an entry porch had been built over that, leading into the hotel kitchen. When 29 year old Fred Meyer walked over the floor with a side of meat on his shoulder the floor gave way. Despite desperate efforts to rescue the young man, the gases of the old well overcame him, and nauseated all who attempted to reach him.

Of course, Crout received the blame for not having put decent flooring over the well, and for not having the well filled up in the first place. Enough was enough for Crout. He sold out to Holliday.

The Frontier stood across the street southeast from the Trabing site, thus putting Trabing, Bannon & Company and Holliday all within spitting distance of each

---

*   Messuage – mess'wij: Referring to main buildings and adjacent outbuildings. There were at least two houses with sheds, and a small barn as part of the Frontier complex. The hotel itself was log, built for the Freemans.

other. The size of their operations would seem too much for so small a community as Laramie, but the Union Pacific Rolling Mills were still operating, there were mines bringing forth ores, timber camps were everywhere in the mountains, ranching was a money-making proposition and much English and other foreign money was coming into the country. In town there were nine or ten hotels and boarding houses, and the town was still swinging with 24 saloons and bars plus gambling dives and various card rooms, although it had slowed down a bit. And the red-light district had expanded and was running wide-open. Business in Laramie City was booming in all directions.

Only a few years after the erection of the three big department stores, Laramie's newspapers (there were several that had published for a time and later retired to oblivion) were extolling the charms and businesses of the Gem City.

They related that there were, by 1890, 7,000 people in the city. In addition to the iron-rolling mills there was a soda reduction works, railroad tie-preserving plants, two planing mills, a window glass factory, railroad machine shops, flouring mill, tannery, brewery (they ignored the numerous two-bit back-lot rectifiers), bottling works for soda pop, an electric light and power plant, (the first in the Rocky Mountain region), a gold quartz stamp mill, plaster mill, a soap factory, telephone exchange, sewer system, mountain spring water works, artesian wells, stone quarries, and brick yards, driving tracks, two daily and weekly newspapers. The State Penitentiary (although that was transferred to Rawlins shortly after), the State University and State Fish Hatchery, two public schools, one parochial (Catholic) school, (the earlier Baptist Seminary had been discontinued), eight churches, three national banks and one loan and trust company. There was a hospital, YMCA reading room, public libraries, a theatre (the Opera

House located atop the Holliday Store had been discontinued by then) and a public park. And the city was looking into the feasibility of a wool-processing plant and a street railway. One editor added after the railway notation "In our eye."

So, when Holliday added his ambitious merchandising business on the corner at Second and South C, there was plenty of business activity in town and country to encourage the great stores in Laramie. Holliday himself continued heavily in the logging business. It provided materials for his sawmill and planing shops which covered the block between Third and Fourth Streets and South E (Kearney) and D (Sheridan). Holliday also operated a building-construction business.

In addition to the practical and utilitarian departments in his store, Holliday had added the opulent Opera House atop his huge building. It was a fine gesture for hoped-for cultural enrichment of the Gem City. Either the residents didn't care for culture or felt they were refined enough, for the opera house wasn't a success and was soon closed. But the great store was a success. It outlasted Trabing's venture by a good half-century, but in 1948 the Holliday complex met the same fate as Trabing's and the blaze destroyed or damaged a fair part of Laramie's business district. The difference between the two great fires was the high wind which fanned the Holliday blaze.

Those winds which periodically raced downslope from the rugged western mountains and scoured across the Laramie Plains caused much comment in neighboring newspapers. Hayford, as usual, had a ready comeback: "Sure Laramie has wind, but not the hard blows that occur elsewhere. At least, we've never had a length of stovepipe blown out of a shanty in Laramie!"

Among the worthy pioneers of Laramie was George W. Fox. Fox was instrumental in getting the Union Pacific company to deed three lots to the Methodist Episcopal Church organization for a building site, and he was one of the charter members of the congregation. This pillar of the church was most helpful to the early pastors, encouraging them when attendance was small and helping to keep a small offering coming into the treasury.

Fox was well appreciated for his faithfulness; however one gentle pastor complained in his diary about the "never-ending gossips of this town" and referred to the troubles of Brother Fox with the same. He did not elaborate for several days' entries when he wrote his private disapproval of that dear brother for squiring about that "shallow, flirtatious demoiselle, Mrs. Smith ..." whose husband was spending time in the penitentiary across the river.

The pastor met the demoiselle at a tea in the home of one of the church members and was not immune to her charms. He confided to his diary that she was quite different from his earlier estimate, that she was ". . . a handsome woman and seemed sweet and considerate, . . . if somewhat giddy . . ." He also added that that night he had written an extra long letter to his wife back in Illinois begging her to hurry her departure to Wyoming.

He also declared he did not believe the gossip of an intimate relationship between the "sweet, considerate lady" and Fox, especially since Fox assured him that none existed.

Young Fox worked for S. R. LeRoy in his 16 by 30-foot tent-hardware store which stood on the alley back of the spot where in earlier days the Big Tent had livened the town. A board shanty had soon replaced the little tent, and in turn had been replaced by a log building.

LeRoy's Hardware Store is said to have been the

meeting place for the Forty Liars of Bill Nye's book "Forty Liars and Other Lies." But then, 's store was also credited with spawning this famous group. There may have been other back rooms where they, or other liars met from time to time as well.

The equivalent of these liars could be found in any country store well into the 20th century as long as the old coal-burning heating stoves were used. It was the ideal place to gather and "spin a few yarns" on any day of the year, with or without a fire in the stove, so long as there was a box of sand to spit into.

Fox met and wed pretty Ellen Blake when she came to Laramie in 1872. This gentle lady lived well into her nineties, lively and with good memory of the early days of the town. Like so many others, however, her memory of occurrences on the town's rowdy front streets had been obscured by those milder, more meaningful happenings in her own social sphere. And in those days "no lady ever ventured near First Street!"

Fox, Mike Quann and a number of other Laramie young blades took a trip to the Dakota gold fields. They all returned to Laramie rather wiser than richer. For a time, then, Fox ran a meat market, with its own slaughterhouse out on the river a couple of miles south of town. When that burned down mysteriously he went to work again for LeRoy and was one of the Forty Liars himself. LeRoy sold his hardware business to Holcomb and Grow, and in 1889 Fox bought them out. The store at that time was housed in "a fine brick block" built by Galusha Grow's father-in-law Edward A. Ivinson.

Fox seemed to be a fine steady man of mild enough deportment who made no big impact on the Laramie scene. He seemed to be one of the thousands of citizens that quietly attend to business and form the foundations of industry in a nation. He had a fine, sweet tenor voice and sang at church functions, funerals, weddings and public events. His usual accompanist was Nancy

Fillmore Brown, wife of Laramie's three-week Mayor. Fox served the community in many areas, including as a juror at different times, a typical, steady citizen.

When he served as juror for the George Cook trial, however, he was so vocal and vicious in condemnation of the shootist one is made to wonder. Maybe his religious beliefs were strictly against drinking or spirits of any kind, although the "sweet and considerate demoiselle" he had earlier squired about town apparently had not been averse to a drink now and again.

When it was made public that the Cook trial had been conducted with an extra juror, Fox was released from the panel. Cook's attorney requested a new trial which was not granted, and the young man was sent to the gallows.

Frontier Hotel, log section is the original 1868 building. Frame addition put up by William Crout, 1870.

Beery Collection.

Patrick Doran and friend Svenson and Patricks red setter.
Picture taken after 1900.

Courtesy of Laramie Plains Museum.

Second location of
Dawson Brothers and
Sutphen Brothers stores,
South A.

Beery Collection.

National Theatre and Old Blue Front.
The Front Street Courthouse. Later Trabing's store and warehouse. Later still, warehouse for The Laramie Grocery Company. This picture taken after 1900. Portion marked "The Laramie" was the original Saloon-Theatre.

Beery Collection.

The Crisman House,
after remodeling
by Noah Worth.

Beery Collection.

The first of the *Sentinel* buildings.
115 Front (First) Street.

Courtesy of Western History Research Center,
University of Wyoming.

Second Street between Centre (University) and South A (Ivinson), 1885. Laramie National Bank on corner, Downey law office left, Sentinel offices (second location) City Hall and Methodist Church.

Courtesy of American Heritage Center, University of Wyoming.

Looking northwest from roof of Holiday store at Second and South C (Garfield). Roofs of Frontier Hotel buildings in foreground. Bannon-Mandell store across street. Trabing's new store; Watkin's Dry Goods; Dr. Finfrock's offices (old site of Alhambra saloon); Kidd's Shoe Store; W. S. Knadler saloon; Bintz Drugs with living quarters above.

Courtesy of Western History Research Center, University of Wyoming.

Typical log home.
Chinked log with clay mud nogging for insulation.
Plastered over noggin' and painted,
usually with buttermilk paint.

Beery Collection.

Murphy's Tammany Hall,
First and Grand, after 1880.

Courtesy of Laramie Civic
Center.

T. D. Abbott Books and Stationery on left. Stephen Downey standing in doorway of furniture store. John Conner's Wyoming Billiard Hall next door, where Rev. J. E. Edmondson preached.

Courtesy of Western History Research Center, University of Wyoming.

Looking southwest across U. P. tracks. Church at left is Scandinavian Lutheran and is still standing.

Courtesy of American Heritage Center, University of Wyoming.

Three

Businesses were flourishing all over town, although still concentrated in the original six-block area. Some were hole-in-the-wall shops such as the harness shop of Anderson and Gilroy on the south side of B Street, next door to Murphy's Saloon (later known as Tammany Hall), or Chris Wille's cubby-hole boot shop in a side room of the Centennial, or even the mysterious K2-Tor restaurant across the street from the old Tivoli.

Businesses were opened with a grand flourish and quietly closed months later. Competition was too stiff. The cafe opened by Mrs. Reese Davis on Front Street lasted a few short months. Susannah Clark had long ago been forced to close her restaurant and had left town. The Last Chance, another two-by-four cafe fared well enough for several years but that may have been because the couple also ran a bakery. The K2-Tor closed at the end of a month, by mutual consent of the partners. This couple, H. H. Richards and Harriet Adele Rice (daughter of Pap and Euphemia Rice, owners of the Tivoli) were married, had a glorious, rousing quarrel, apparently over their new two-room brick house which had suffered a mechanic's lien filed for money due. H. H. left Harriet with the lien to satisfy and moved to rooms downtown. Harriet filed for divorce on charges of desertion. When, a few years later, Pap and Emia Rice moved to Walden, Harriet went along. H. H. moved to Walden, too, in 1883, but he and Harriet didn't renew their relationship, so far as is known. The K2Tor stood across the alley from Nellie Wright's well-patronized Crystal Wine Parlors. Perhaps it was too close and Nellie lured away potential customers.

The Oyster Bar fared very well, first under management of Johnny Dimmitt, known as Oyster Johnny, and later with Jennie McCall.

Jennie's business ability was widely praised. Even the knowledge that she had "upstairs girls" (which enhanced her business) brought no complaint.

Eateries which served "refreshments" seemed to fare better, but most of the ordinaries served only food. The consuming passions of the work force around Laramie varied widely and drinking men clearly preferred the company of other manly elbow benders.

George P. Goldacker's log and frame building, raised in 1870, was also known as Goldacker's Hairdressing Saloon. It was the town's first public bath house after running water was brought to the downtown stores. Advertisements boast: "Soap, brushes, sponges and towels furnished. First class bath - 50¢."

After dissolving partnership with brother-in-law Ludolph Abrams in their several properties, Henry Bath bought Goldacker out and put up a "brick block with iron and stone front" which he called the Humboldt House. It became one of the most popular boarding houses in town and stood next north of the old Diana.

Bath, called "a natural Boniface" for his cheerful and accommodating manner, held a grand Christmas party with a select group to celebrate the opening of his new business. The party was a quiet affair according to prevailing standards in the town, and possibly because the businessmen brought their wives. It may have been at this celebration that one lively German matron exhibited her ability to "kick the chandelier." This probably didn't reach the ears of the *Sentinel*, for the paper praised the apparent growing sophistication of the town. Even the 1883 New Year's celebration held at the Humboldt by the Maennorchor Society with food, choice drink and lively songfest ended with all heads intact, if somewhat confused. Probably further evidence of sophistication.

The Humboldt House operated for a good ten years under the Bath hand. In 1891 John Keane, the old pioneer whose first log house at Third and Custer had served as gallows for Asa Moore and friends, bought the Humboldt, re-dressed and re-named it and advertised it as the "Gem City Hotel, a family hotel serving choicest wines, foods and room accommodations in homelike atmosphere." It continued its quiet operation, just about the only quiet hotel other than Childs' to operate in Laramie.

The New York House had a more colorful career.

In 1870 Ludolph Abrams and Henry Bath built the wooden New York House on First Street. It was not their first business venture in town. The pair had earlier operated a restaurant with billiard rooms a block north. That business was known as the American Restaurant which the partners sold to Fred Hesse and George Ritter.

Abrams, as did all early settlers in Laramie, owned several properties and seemed to be constantly buying and selling. The New York House was one property that he hung onto throughout the years, possibly because of a mineral spring on the back of the lots. He may have hoped to one day make a bit of money from it. As it was, he had fresh flowing water for his business and eventually he put in a "monster cistern" for storage. There is no evidence that he tried to increase custom by exploiting the wonderful water. Nor is there ever mention of a back-lot brewery at his place, although there may have been. These "rectifiers" seldom advertised their wares in the newspapers.

The New York House was advertised as inviting and comfortable, as were all hotels in town, and it, too, had its "Sample Room to accommodate commercial men."

Abrams followed the course taken by other inn-keepers and rented out the business from time to time. Sometimes it was only the bar that was leased, other times it was the whole lay-out. The first lease of record was for a year to Charles Kuster, often referred to as "Old Kooster," while he and Tom Sanders were still leasing the blue-painted National Theatre from the first Mrs. August Trabing.

The second experience of note was in 1878. Abrams leased to John Huempfner who gave the place a thorough overhauling and wrought "wonderful changes through the labyrinth of rooms." The *Sentinel* reports that Huempfner placed a "15-ball pool table in the public room" and decorated the dining room in baby-blue. No mention is made of the impact the color may have had on trade.

At his grand opening Huempfner issued and invitation in German for "every singer and friend of singing" to come and join in a singing club. Apparently there was never a formal singing group until the Maennerchoer Society was organized some years later.

On the boardwalk in front of the New York House on a bright, sunny and very cold Thanksgiving Day in 1883 young James Blount, janitor at the East Side schoolhouse, died ingloriously at the hand of his wife's brother, George Cook.

Cook, who worked at the U. P. sheds in Medicine Bow, had come by train to Laramie to spend the holiday with his sister and Blount and "have a good time." Both men had spent the day drinking and prowling the town, arguing, joking, having another sip, and quarreling. And finally Cook, age 23, had shot Blount.

The victim was the father of four children plus a four-day old baby, and the "wilful, malicious, dastardly deed" had raised every hackle in town.

Hayford inveighed at length in his newspaper columns against drinking and those who drank, and openly suggested hanging. Cook, he reasoned, "was worthless, had few friends and was of no account." Other townspeople argued and discussed the act on the streets, giving foundation to the argument by defense that there could be no fair trial in Laramie due to prejudice. Fox was among those voicing opinions on the subject. Preachers preached lengthy sermons against John Barleycorn and strongly urged every one to sign temperance pledge cards. Cook was hanged in effigy before the New York House, scene of the shooting. A torch-light parade preceded the effigy-hanging. Cook stood trial of questionable fairness and a year later, on December 12, 1884, was hanged in the yard of Albany County's courthouse.

Editor Hayford was among those invited by Cook to witness his hanging. The editor did not go. He took the story of the execution from the Rawlins newspaper's pages.

On December first, 1883, the New York House, in toto, was leased to one Brainard Miller and formally re-named the "Wyoming Hall." Miller's reputation as an operator promised a "well-run house ...." Abrams may have been glad to get out of the business after the Cook affair for a few years later he sold out to Ben Watkins and the old place remained in the public eye under a different flag.

As the town grew and railroad travel increased, and the homestead parcels were opened, more and more people came west drawn by the wild mystique of the frontier. Homesteads were taken up and settlers were plentiful. The newcomers fanned out over the valley and great grassy plains to the waiting lands.

Those who wished could hold onto their homesteads, prove up and receive patents. Many didn't stay long enough for that but relinquished their claims for a few dollars and moved on to what seemed a more promising location. Or they didn't want to stay and fight the severe winters that plague this land of long horizons. Many lacked funds to remain. Those who did stay ran cattle or sheep or horses. Grass was plentiful, even if it did take many acres to graze one cow. Horse ranchers had a good thing going, for that was the only mode of travel besides the train, which not everyone could afford. It was with the many horse-ranchers that Bronco Sam, the dusky cowboy from Texas-way, gained his fame as a horse-breaker. Any horse "handled" by Sam brought a good price.

Some of the settlers made good. Some didn't. They all worked and saved in the accepted tradition of "I can do it!" and their work and sweat sometimes balanced out.

The habitues on the front streets of Laramie now included a mixture of miners, railroaders, mill hands, trail hands and cowboys and sheepherders. Fort Sanders had been abandoned in 1882 and soldiers no longer haunted the streets of Laramie.

One nameless shepherd in from his lonely job acquired unexpected publicity when he got "happy" and began to "hoo-raw" the occupants of Ben Watkins' Wyoming Hall. The result was a few sore heads and swollen noses, a lot of broken furniture and one large plate-glass window. The sheepherder was unharmed and unidentified, but he made the acquaintance of the judge, meekly paid his fine and returned to the campwagon and his flock, flat broke and still happy.

As for the Watkins joint: it came under closer scrutiny of the law. Ben, himself no stranger to the bottle, tangled with Policeman Morgan Knadler, a big German ex-soldier standing 6-foot-4 inches in size-14 shoes and tipping the scale at 250 pounds.

It began with some heavy words shortly after the sheepherder's spree, and Watkins told Knadler what he could do with his badge and gave battle when the policeman tried to arrest him. They wrestled to the floor and Knadler finally had to choke the wiry Watkins into submission before he could handcuff him. Another big window was broken and furniture broken and Watkins landed in jail. He paid a ten-dollar fine and was released. A short while later Knadler returned to the Wyoming Hall, accompanied by Policeman Johnson and another row followed. This time Watkins spent the night in jail and was put under a $50 peace bond. No reason was given for the officer's second visit. The newspaper commented dryly that a good deal of booze was mixed up in the affair.

Watkins sold out not long afterward, and a few years later a brick building was raised on the spot. One reminder of the old randy days is the beautiful pressed-tin ceiling in the still sturdy building which now houses an antiques shop.

꩜ꆞ꩜ꆞ꩜

One of the few quiet dispensaries in town was that of Michael H. Murphy. He, like so many others, had quiet back rooms for gaming. His saloon, which stood at 301 First (Front) Street, became known as Tammany Hall, probably because it became a popular forum for political debates. M. H. did a fair amount of "shylocking" on the side. There were plenty of candidates with something to pawn for a drink. Or a meal and bed. People needed a sympathetic place to go after Patrick Doran lost his beloved Shamrock to unpaid taxes and mortgages. Murphy took his friend in to tend bar at the Tammany. Without doubt the blackboard never hung behind the Murphy bar, and Doran was under strict orders not to "wipe the slate clean" for anyone. Murph, at least, prospered moderately well in his business.

As if there were not enough sales being made in the two dozen grogshops, liquors and wines were to be had at most of the regular grocery and provision stores. C. S. Dunbar advertised St. Louis Lager, and Trabing's ads

53

listed a dozen or more fine brands. The Trabing brothers made their own backyard German beer for a number of years.

It is a question whether it was Trabings' spirits which Hayford referred to when he mentioned the brewer who put Wisconsin labels on his products. The Trabings had deep family ties in Wisconsin as was well-known about town.

"Polite drinks" could also be had in places other than in saloons where the serious perpendicular drinking was done. And there were, in addition, liquids of many varieties to be found in the clubs and card-rooms where gambling was also serious.

Among the numerous gaming rooms were Club 11 (Eleven) in upstairs parlors on South A; the Orleans, which advertised "Keno nightly"; the higher class Gurney and Cleveland Club which occupied the old Tivoli for a time and then moved to other quarters in the same block. There was gaming in quiet side rooms in various hotels away from the parlors where lady travelers might sit, and carry-in drinks were served there if players wished. And of course they did.

If there weren't enough places for social drinking, new ones were opened up or old ones re-cycled periodically. The Old Capitol was one of those re-opened by a man named Pettus who always "served the boys right royally" — for a while. Three months after opening Pettus was gone and Tom Skelly was re-fitting the Capitol on borrowed money. That went royally, too, until November when Skelly was in need of money to meet his mortgage. He headed out to raise some. When last seen he was reported in Ogden "headed west and still going." Perhaps the location of the Old Capitol was to blame for not drawing trade. But there were others around to fill the void left by the Capitol.

Handsome Morris Newman was one rendering that service. He sold his beer at 5 cents a schooner with free oyster stew. It is not revealed how he managed his generosity, and somehow had engaged in argument with the Laramie Times for "casting odium on him." Perhaps questioning how he could be so generous. At any rate, the quarrel lasted for some time but finally it was patched up over a schooner or two of beer and Hayford reported that the handsome publican had forgiven the Times and "continued to wave as he passed their offices."

"Oh, where is the Spirit of '76?" the Fourth of July orator cried.

"It's all drunk up," floated back the reply from out in the crowd.

All too true. As true as the old poem, author unknown, which lasted well into the 20th century:

"He is not drunk who from the floor

Can arise and drink once more,

But he is drunk who prostrate lies

And can neither drink nor rise."

J. J. Fein, an enterprising Dutchman, advertised the opening of his brewery in German, inviting "all good fellows on July 4th to a festival in honor of the day for one lively time —"

Fein ran the first Delmonico restaurant in town. (Twenty years later George Phillips used the same name for his beanery. It is now a part of the Senior Center on First Street.) J. J. operated his Delmonico on the east side of Second Street. Back of the restaurant stood his City Brewery, adjacent to another rectifier belonging to Clausen & Company.

Fein and Fred Bath set up a partnership for one year on a 50-50 basis. Their agreement states that Bath was to act as brewer and Fein had no say in the business except to inspect and suggest. Since Fein had his own opinions, the easiest way for him to abide by that agreement was to stay out of town. This he did and spent much of that year out in the Snowy Range prospecting for gold. He found some. He also found a coal mine. Evidently Fein's "find" was enticing, for when the partnership with Bath ended, Fred took out for the hills himself. What his luck may have been was undisclosed, but upon his return to town he opened up a brewery of his own over by the river bridge with a fine beer garden and a rousing good time. He ran carriage service so the gents could bring their ladies to the garden. A German band provided drinking and dancing music.

Fein re-opened his own back-lot works. Then the revenue officers descended because a big row had been kicked up over frauds of a "whiskey ring" and some said the crooked whiskey was being traced to Laramie. So Fein was in trouble with the Government. He was charged, too, with neglecting and refusing to keep a Brewer's Book as required by law. The revenuers accused J. J. with attempt to defraud the government and his Hayford-rating plummeted to zero. The editor published the fall court proceedings with the following remarks:

> The criminal business is pretty much over for this term . . . The only conviction so far is of Jake Fein for his awkward, irregular method of bookkeeping. We have no idea what will be done to Jake but we hope he will be hung, drawn and quartered . . . This abominable, loose habit . . . of bookkeeping demands that somebody should be made an example of and we don't know of anyone the world could spare better than Jake.

Jake's piety may have been deeper than Hayford's, for he did not make the retort he could have. Nor did he withdraw his advertising from the *Sentinel* as others did when caught under Hayford's teaspoonful of mud.

Fein paid a fine of $300 and soon afterward his advertisements resumed in the newspaper. Translated from the German the first read:

> Attention Company! Jake Fein will open the Brewery, that great resort of good fellows, tomorrow night. Best of wines,

liquors and cigars will be dispensed over the bar. Music by the Silver Cornet Band. All requested to come and join the chorus. Free lunch and all other good things.

Later on J. J. again leased the brewery and turned the management of the Delmonico Restaurant over to his wife Barbara and he went back to the gold fields and the coal mine he had found. In addition he ran a freight wagon and a stage line to the Snowy Range diggings. He never did get rich.

Things worked a bit differently for George W. Ritter who was elected Treasurer of Albany County.

Ritter was also a restaurateur "meals at all hours-50 cents." It was soon apparent that this was no way to make a fortune, there were too many food dispensaries, so he and J. Fred Hesse became partners. Even the combination saloon/billiard parlor with the American Restaurant didn't line their pockets with the desired lucre, nor did the very desirable Front Street location help.

Hesse apparently did not fret. He had remained in the background of the partnership, even allowing George to advertise their enterprise as "Ritter's Restaurant." Perhaps Ritter's lifestyle was more demanding than Hesse's.

It could, of course, have been that the glitter of County funds was too tempting. At any rate Ritter took a Christmas vacation and it was quickly learned that $16,000 in county money had gone along.

Sheriff J. R. Brophy promptly offered $1,000 (county funds) for information regarding Ritter's whereabouts and return. His description of the man was short and candid:

Said George W. Ritter is about 45 years old, about 5'8, weighs about 145 lbs; has dark complexion, small features, light blue, weak eyes; upper teeth false, recently applied. When he left he had a moustache.

Ritter was found in Denver, returned with most of the money and no moustache, and stood trial. He was sentenced to one year "over the river" in the Territorial Prison on the west bank of the Big Laramie River. He served eleven months (one month off for good behavior), and Governor Thayer issued a pardon. Ritter was welcomed home to Laramie with open arms and resumed his old place among polite society, but not in public office.

At a later time when another County Treasurer was found with public funds clinging to his fingers, he was branded a thief and not let off so lightly. At the same time, however, the County Attorney, member of one of Laramie's prominent families, was found "neglectful" when it was learned that he had not turned in fines that he had collected. His laxity was laid to "carelessness." That, apparently, was only a laughing matter.

Four

When Doctor J. H. Finfrock left Fort Halleck with the buildings which were recycled to make up Fort Sanders, he too was re-cycled. He continued as physician-surgeon with the army only until the arrival of the Union Pacific railroad. A short time after the town was established Finfrock mustered out of the army and became official railroad doctor. His sphere of action was the railroad's tent hospital over on Second Street between Centre and South A (Ivinson).

Then the railroad put up their big new medical building, a two-story frame affair with fewer than a dozen windows, and Finfrock worked there until it was discontinued by the railroad in the fall of 1870. Finfrock then took it over as his private hospital.

The wooden building stood in the railroad yards just west of and between the main line and the side tracks near South F Street (Sheridan).

Patients must have been so ill or wounded they weren't bothered by the noises of passing trains. And the U. P. line was a busy one. At that time, of course, no one went to the hospital except as a last resort. News that someone was in the hospital was always greeted with gravest expectations, for it usually meant the patient was close to death. Whenever someone walked out under his own power, it was a great victory.

One thing in favor of the railroad hospital, it was on the scene of numerous accidents, the cars and railroad shops, so the patient hadn't far to go for help.

Finfrock, as a surgeon during the Civil War, was used to injuries of every type, and illnesses of all degrees. So far as treatment went, frontier doctors used bleeding and in dire emergency, amputations. Surgery was done with no anesthesia other than oversize doses of whiskey or "biting the bullet." Frontier doctors dealt mostly with gunshot wounds and injuries from fistfights or knives, snake bite or broken bones. Children were usually treated by their mothers, unless she felt incompetent. Babies were delivered by midwife, usually.

In ancient time women doctors were considered witches, and this frowning-upon lived on into the 1800's. They treated their own families, nevertheless. Their home-made remedies were generally effective. They used herbs and often roadside weeds. The knowledge of their medicines passed from neighbor to neighbor, from mother to daughter, and still holds a place in modern pharmacology. Ergot was often used. Belladonna was found useful when miscarriage threatened. Digitalis was used, and still is, in treating heart ailments. These, as well as many others are still used in medical treatments.

Women served as mid-wives while "regular" doctors continued their heroic treatments of bleeding, administering huge doses of laxatives, calomel (a laxative containing mercury) and opium. Lay practitioners used herbs, dietary changes and sympathy. Sympathy and the art of listening was often quite effective. One great advantage the family doctor had was that he knew his patients, many from birth or early childhood, and this created a special relationship of trust and respect which may have been more beneficial than the medicine.

Mostly, of course, folks treated themselves, especially if they lived at a distance from a doctor. Folk remedies were found reliable, and patent medicines were heavily depended on. The worse it smelled or tasted, the "better it was for you."

Doctors, of course, were really expensive. They charged 25¢ or 50¢ for house calls or office calls, and as much as one dollar for a house call if they had to stay the night. Payment was often "in kind" such as food, fuel, meat, sometimes even kittens or puppies. They even accepted promises to pay. There wasn't much hard cash on hand.

A number of doctors were working in Laramie off and on during those early years, but for much of that time the main ones were Doctors Finfrock, Harris, Latham and Dysart. Others of more or less popularity and skill came later. Finfrock ran a drugstore for a number of years. He had Louis Thobro as partner when they operated the Eagle Pharmacy on Second Street. Later Gramm bought Thobro out, and after several years, bought out Finfrock's interest. Otto Gramm became a prominent figure in the business and civic circles of Laramie City.

Even though the early frontier doctor had all the "learnin'" available to him, it remained that he still "practiced" medicine. And, of course, he was allowed to bury his mistakes.

One of these mistakes was uncovered by happenchance when the city cemetery had to be moved.

The first burials of pioneers were made on railroad land away out of town on Sixth to Eighth Streets, covering one and a half blocks. When the city expanded eastward, the railroad company saw opportunity to sell that particular property, so asked the city to transfer burials to another site. This was done in the spring of 1872 with city jail-birds doing the manual labor, and village teamsters doing the hauling.

All went well until the workmen unearthed a casket that required the efforts of four hefty, well-muscled men. None of the other caskets had required such efforts, so out of curiosity the men opened the casket.

Inside they found the corpse of a man named Elias Kerr, a popular young lawyer, well-known about town, but a hopeless drunk. The corpse, instead of lying on its back with hands folded across the chest in the accepted position, was lying face down in the casket, and it was colored a peculiar blue. It was also turned to stone.

Jim Sherrod, one of the teamsters, related that he had whetted his knife on the stone thigh and got a good edge, too.

Speculation ran high when the discovery was made. The workmen recalled that Kerr had died less than two years previously of what the doctor called "delirium tremens." The workmen also recalled that Kerr had been sweet on the doctor's daughter and the "old man" had been decidedly against the match. A coroner's jury had been called in when Kerr died, and returned a verdict of "death by accidental overdosage on the part of the patient." Since medicine had been left on the bedside stand by the doctor, it was surmised Kerr had taken too much in his delirium.

Now, looking at the blue stone corpse which lay in such an unusual position, it was speculated that Kerr had not been dead when he was buried. Of course, they thought he had come to and in his struggle for air had turned over. But, the body could have turned over while being lowered into the pit. But what would have caused it to turn to stone? A combination of booze and drugs? No other casket held a stone corpse, so it was nothing in the soil, they thought, that might have caused the circumstance. So it probably was an instance of a doctor "practicing" his medicine.

❧❧❧❧❧

Sanitation in those early days was given little thought. Even in this country's first public hospital, started in New York City in 1736 and called Bellevue, sanitation was given scant attention. In the late 1870's a committee investigating the hospital could not find a single bar of soap on the premises. This is the institution where Henry Wagner went for study and was awarded a Certificate of Doctor of Medicine.

For a subject so little considered by doctors, it was small wonder then, that early towns carried such a high aroma. Laramie was no different.

Water was hauled from the Laramie River and peddled around town, sold by bucket or barrel and stored in tanks or other receptacle. For household use, other than cooking or drinking, there was the rain-barrel, which, due to the dry climate was seldom full. Morgan Knadler and Jacob Fein, two members of the large German colony in Laramie, operated their own private water wagons.

It is not known where they filled their tanks, but two miles upstream stood a slaughter house with attendant feedyards, and three brick yards operated on the river's edge closer in to town. The nearest, of course, was the Territorial Prison directly west of town.

Springs east of the village furnished a good head of water which Henry Wagner, N. F. Spicer and Ira Pease and others diverted to town use. Open ditches bordered the dirt streets and the flowing water was handy for everyone, householders and businesses alike. Barrels were sunk in the ditches for household use, but often left uncovered. Many a party-bound lady or gent stepped from their buggy in the unlighted street and into a water barrel with sad effect on their evening finery.

Cattle, pigs, chickens and dogs roamed the streets at will, so the open ditches saw much use by them as well as by the children playing in the water. Before the Union Pacific company and town officials began piping water from the springs in 1874 there arose hue and cry to get the livestock out of the streets. Straining and boiling the river and ditch water was not made a regular practice, if at all. The result was much illness. Epidemics of typhoid were not unusual.

Table scraps, dishwater, bath and wash and scrub water all were thrown into the backyards and every lot had its privy. Many residents owned a milk cow and a few chickens, and more owned a saddle horse or driving pair so a barn and its companion manure pile added their flavors to the town. It was all natural and accepted and not to be sniffed at.

With the innovation of piped water the populace were beginning to consider the finer things in life. Homemakers' work was lightened by carrying water from certain street corner hydrants instead of dipping from water-barrels.

A bath house, established on West Front Street, and the East Front Street Bath Rooms which George Goldacker installed in his hairdressing salon, helped to lift part of the high-spirited aroma hovering over Laramie.

Goldacker soon left Laramie for Cheyenne where he was subsequently elected coroner of Laramie County, probably a more exciting task than emptying someone's bath water.

In private homes, the galvanized tin wash tub still served for bathing. In winter the performance took place close to the kitchen stove or a heating stove in the "front" room.

City officials began levying fines against owners who allowed their livestock to run loose. The water ditches were cleaned more often and it might be said that civilization had at last reached Laramie.

The advent of the railroad's rolling mills and shops brought more than 500 new residents to town. They needed housing so the building business boomed. W.H. Holliday had moved one of his planing mills from Sherman town to Laramie in 1872 when he was awarded the contract to build the Territorial Prison. His planing and building operation soon covered an entire block in Laramie City, and the screeching of saws combined with those of Titus Weber's mill rent the air daily. The whine of hand-saws, thumping of hammers, scolding of train engines and their screaming whistles further assaulted the clear air of the great Laramie Valley.

The millhands required housing and they didn't quibble over quality. They took what was available. Anywhere along the alleys could be found shack or cabin once used as bar or crib or dwelling before the riff-raff had moved out in '68. With those gone, others had moved into the buildings, or even hauled a building to a more desirable location. As people were able to afford better quarters in better areas (and much quieter), they didn't hesitate to move away from the alleys and backways and many of those early places were left empty and cold. And dirty.

On occasion the newspapers reported that an "element of half-grown boys and whiskey-soaked bums" were having blow-outs on Sundays, and sometimes *even during the week* ! . . . "at two joints along the alley paralleling Front Street."

The "elements" had fixed up an old abandoned shack or two where they met to "play cards, drink beer or other intoxicants, plot against virtue and perhaps to lay plans for robbing hen roosts, potato patches and clothes lines."

A group of such bums was collected by sheriff Colford from a shack behind the old Shamrock and fined for vagrancy and drunkenness. City officials, aggravated by citizen complaints over having to house and feed these "bums" finally put them to cleaning the streets (horse traffic was heavy) and water ditches on the premise that having to work would make them leave town. More often than not the bums left, leaving the officials to brag that they had given them the "bum's rush."

Five

The odium attached to Front Street apparently did not go beyond Centre Street for a number of the more prominent townspeople built rather fine, comfortable homes north of that dividing line. The respectable Rolling Mill Hotel and Adams' House were the only early businesses to appear north of Centre. Later the Atlantic boarding house at Third and Lewis operated until it burned down.

All activity was not confined to East Front Street, however. There was quite a fuss made when Jack Evans, a cowboy from the Little Laramie Valley rode his horse into a west side saloon and crowded patrons from the bar. No one was hurt but the cowboy was made to pay a stiff fine of $5 for racing his horse up and down West Front and "scaring women and little children."

As stated previously, the original Front Street faced the tracks and ran from Centre Street south to F (Sheridan). Between the tracks and the river, all that area north of Centre was open land until it was patented as Henry Hodgeman's homestead.

When the Union Pacific put town lots up for sale in 1868 the townsite was on land legally a part of the Fort Sanders Military Reserve. It was not until 1875 when the reservation was reduced and the railroad company gained title to the land that buyers had clear title to lots they had bought years before. So there were many illegal squatters.

Hodgeman was granted patent to the area between Centre and Sheridan, and Michael Carroll immediately petitioned the Land Office to recall that patent, claiming it had been obtained by misrepresentation, falsehood and fraud. And Carroll warned that persons should not purchase from Hodgeman any portion of the west half of the southeast quarter of Section thirty two, Township 16, Range 73. This, of course, was Carroll's own homestead.

The Union Pacific railroad advertised those lots for sale where illegal squatters thought they owned. The advertisement and notice appeared in the *Sentinel*:

> "Those parties occupying Union Pacific lots for which they have not paid are warned that they must settle immediately or run the risk of having their houses sold with the lots to other parties."

The company published that notice with the caution to "either buy the lots you occupy or move the buildings or forfeit them."

Hodgeman had his 40-acre homestead platted and offered lots for sale in his "Hodgeman's Addition," and adopted the same tactic used by the railroad. His orders to squatters to either pay or move and forfeit were not kindly received. Some found no other recourse so paid his price. Others balked.

On December 10, eight days after his lots were advertised and the edict issued, Hodgeman accosted Frank Moir, machinist at the railroad shops, and requested $500 for the lot which Moir occupied.

Moir had put up a fine brick building with yard and fences nicely laid out. It probably excited covetous feelings in the eye of many a beholder. Moir read the announcement and decided he would not pay the $500. He had already taken down the fences and was on a scaffold tearing down the house brick by brick when Hodgeman showed up.

Moir refused to pay the fine and Hodgeman saw that fine house going down bit by bit. He began to rave and "cuss out" Moir and threw bricks at the man on the scaffold. One missile hit Moir in the head cutting quite a gash. That gentleman threw his hand-axe at Hodgeman (which missed) and followed the tool to the ground. The two men then engaged in a "pounding match."

Later Moir went to Dr. Harris for a patch-up of his wounds, then to see an attorney. Hodgeman was arrested for assault and battery. His fine, plus costs was $24.

Moir gathered up all his building materials and built a new house out on South B (Grand) between Ninth and Tenth Streets.

By this time the town had expanded east and west. Wilson's two-story hotel over on the west side of the tracks was completed and ready to accommodate a large number of guests. Competition over there was brisk. Wilson's house stood on Garfield, the main road out of town and over the river. Wilcox and the others were nearer the center of railroad activity north of Garfield.

Out on tenth street, just east of the new schoolhouse stood the ornate house that Peter Holt had built for his recalcitrant bride. Financial reverses caused him to lose "Holt's Folly" and it was now owned and occupied by Judge I. P. Caldwell.

The block and a half, once occupied by the city cemetery, was now being built up with fine residences. Matthew Dawson had built an impressive two-story "mansion" for his attractive young bride, the former Jennie Fillmore. And the banker Balch had built a smaller, but just as elegant cottage on the lots south of Dawson. Across the street south stood the big, hulking East Side School.

When that site was settled on for the schoolhouse, one of the main objectors was Editor Hayford. "We might as well build it in Cheyenne!" he fumed in the *Sentinel*. Later, of course, he expounded at length on the new building and the excellent selection of teachers who were to direct the learning of the young students.

Six

The old English pub or "ordinary," and later the taverns and inns in Colonial America were forerunners of the saloon with bar and brass foot-rail which has become the accepted fixture in any tale about the American frontier.

Successive waves of Irish and German immigrants brought to American shores a horde of accustomed drinkers. The liquor industry grew, and the skill of the bartender grew with it. He could mix any concoction, give it a fancy name and start a new fad. The remark was made by someone that the corkscrew was the most effective instrument for letting fun show up in people.

Along with the brew, local gossip was dispensed, special days and traditions were observed and toasted. The quick were discussed and frequently cussed. The dead were praised, faintly at times, for on such occasions all mortals face their own eternity, so generous works flowed with the cup o' kindness.

The toasting of traditions and holidays was always done, and buying a round was an unquestioned bit of drinking etiquette. By the time everyone had observed that privilege the glow was warm and personal and the orbit high. Failure to buy, even in your own dramshop could have severe consequences.

To this tradition several men-about-town could agree. One fellow refused to set 'em up because of the presence of too many free-loaders and for several days nursed an oversize nose and other bruises for his negligence.

Charlie Kuster "tried to kick the stuffin' outa" Frederick Bense when the latter accused him of wrong dealing at cards and then refused to buy Bense a round of lager. The pair appeared before Judge I. P. Caldwell who found "Kooster" guilty and fined him one dollar plus costs. The reporter blamed the "Teutonic extraction" of the two men as reason for their strong tempers.

There were tempers other than German, however. When a couple of Irishmen began to argue over their cups, one made some too-personal remarks and the other pulled his gun which discharged into the ceiling as it was drawn.

After a "vigorous investigation" by police, charges filed against the would-be shootist were withdrawn and the pair returned to the drinks. All arguments weren't settled so amicably.

The all-evil idea of saloons has been foolishly laid to the "farmer mentality" of the period. It may be remembered that the temperance movement was not started by any farmer.

Excesses followed naturally in the wake of an evening of drinking and the results were easy to predict: bottle plus tippling equals argument followed by truculence plus action equals battle.

In one of these actions one Fred Lemmy was arraigned for being drunk and on the warpath. The tale, as reported in the *Sentinel* bears the imprint of Bill Nye:

> Hizoner said the City Ordinance doesn't specify what *warpath* is. Complainant changed to *rambunctious* and said that Lemmy had tossed a stone at him, and if he hadn't dodged he wouldn't be here today.

> Lemmy looked sad, wearing watch-pockets at the corner of his forehead, with eye in heavy mourning. He was fined $9.50, paid by Lemmy's employer who related that Lemmy had had a hard childhood, was the victim of a vicious step-pa, had been early cast upon the world and cold charities of the flowing bowl.

Nye sharpened his wit with the following exposition:

> John Daley of Cheyenne was charged by Murphy with a quart bottle and otherwise disturbing the Murph. Both men

apparently had been attacked by quart bottles during the day . . . the principal witnesses were Messrs. Fee and Fein. It is not to be wondered therefore that fees and fines have been the judgement. The charge though was changed to simple assault and battery. Daley eats breakfast in the restaurant at the county court house now. Murphy continues on his way.

The truculence was demonstrated time and again in fist fights which led to arrests and fines. Surprisingly, the largest fine ever levied for fighting was the one Judge Donnellan drew against the "genial boniface" Henry Bath for assault and battery. Bath pleaded guilty to the charge and paid $25 plus costs amounting to $50. The *Sentinel* expressed approval: "If this case should be taken as a precedent and the price of fights established at $50 each, we should soon have the most peaceable community in the country."

The quietest drinking place in town continued to be the Mike Murphy joint at 301 First Street, right in the middle of the red-light district of Laramie. Mike's advertised motto was "Live and Let Live." His specialty was "None but Strictly Pure Goods . . . Choicest Wines for Medicinal Use." That alone should have kept the town in the best of health.

In one of the "can't" of the "can-or-can't" ordinances on Sunday closing of saloons and gambling rooms, the City Council pushed through an ordinance agreeing to license gambling and having open Sundays.

One Councilman was absent and the effort would have gone unnoticed, more or less, except for the Mayor.

N. F. Spicer had campaigned and been elected on the platform of anti-gambling and Sunday closings. He remembered (or was reminded of) his "sworn duty" and vetoed the measure. The Council tried to steam-roller the ordinance through by overriding the veto but failed. This angered some of the council members and their special friends.

The morning after that council meeting found his honorable effigy swinging from a First Street telegraph pole. The Council faced the wrath of an outraged city and quickly called a meeting and passed a resolution denouncing the insult to the Mayor and outrage on the community "by unknown persons."

In order to keep all saloons available for license, the proprietors had never been averse to a little honest graft, nor were the operators of bawdy houses. This is apparent in the careful scrutiny of jurors in trials of certain night-crawlers along the front streets.

Judges had ready answers for their decisions. In one case when Judge Donnellan heard the *City of Laramie versus Peter Thom* for violating the Sunday closing law, he acquitted the defendant. His premise was that Sunday custom was essential because of the number of weekenders who were good spenders, which in turn affected all other businesses in town.

The battle over Sunday closings continued to rise with each successive election.

During one term of "enforcement" Old Kooster was fined for non-compliance and strongly protested. "That door must be left unlocked", he shouted, because his family lived upstairs and they had to have access. This did not explain, however, why the door from hall to barroom was left unlocked. He paid a mild fine for using obscene and abusive language. The door was left unlocked.

Every appearance in court of J. J. Fein was completed by his paying "to the limit of the law" plus costs. Fein was apparently not a person whose successes covered his sins. Among those vigorously protesting the Sunday closings was another German, Wilhelm Fischer, who also paid for making overly-forceful remarks in court. None of these fines were excessive. There were many cases involving the use of abusive and obscene (or provocative) language even before Owen Wister wrote his famous line which supposedly set off Wyoming's "Son of a Bitch" phase.

It was about this time that Fischer's pants were robbed while he slept. It was no secret about town that he left the side door to the family apartment unlocked so midnight customers could waken him. He ran a 24-hour service as did some other businesses. Fischer's specialty was oyster stew.

Fischer kept his trousers draped over a chair handy to pull on when a night customer dropped in. The amount taken was some $70.

The alarm went out over the telegraph wire. This resulted in apprehension of two drifters named Harris and Griffiths at a saloon in Sherman town. They had attracted considerable attention by their plentiful funds and continued arguments. When arrested for questioning each accused the other. They had much of the money left in their pockets when they were brought back to Laramie and lodged in jail to await trial.

Somehow they got one half of a pair of shears and honed it to a dagger point. Their probable intention was to dig out of jail or gain freedom by threatening an officer, but the pair fell to arguing again and Griffiths used the dagger on his accomplice's liver. Harris died and Griffiths went to prison instead of to his home back east.

The death of any man, while tragic and regrettable, didn't create as much sensation as the death of a good ox or horse. The animals represented life or death to any westerner and his family. It made the difference between being able to travel or being stranded, and in the case of the ox, a matter of food.

Seven

The fast and busy life in Laramie City affected not just that on the front streets of the town, but touched every facet of living. At the request of his priest, the organist at the Catholic Church placed an ad in the Sentinel requesting all choir members to attend mass.

The Sentinel reported that so much more rioting, drinking and brawling than usual was going on that no one could be arrested because there was no room in the jail, a 24-by-12 foot affair. Nevertheless with this additional unrest (for which no explanation was given) a group of twenty-four men was sworn in by the County Commissioners as peacekeeping deputies. This apparently had the desired effect for within a few weeks the deputies were all "sworn out" and released from duty.

With this variety of spice and gamey life in Laramie City, it is not surprising that no eyebrow was raised when Noah Wallis' barn was stolen away. Wallis remarked he would be waiting with his Henry rifle when the thieves returned for the foundation.

The Wyoming Legislators at last faced the fact that something should be done state-wide about the liquor problem, if not for their generation, then certainly for their children.

The question had been left to the individual towns and Laramie and Evanston had tried to enforce Sunday closings with off-and-on success as has been noted. Other towns in the Territory had run wide open.

With this decision weighing heavily on their consciences the Territorial Legislature set out to attend a conference on temperance in Salt Lake City.

A Cheyenne paper reported that the salons very thoughtfully provided themselves with enough spirits to see them through the entire excursion.

Many of the rousing activities around town didn't occur on any of the front streets but still involved the Streets' denizens.

John Colford and Larry Fee seem to have been good crowd pleasers on both sides of the political fence. They served as City Marshall as often as there were elections.

In the early years Fee had been a Deputy when Jack Watkins left his calling card (a bullet) in the Fee leg. He was Marshall when one sad and wiser young woman killed her illegitimate baby, then committed suicide. The father of the child, a drifter, had been remorseful and had confessed to Fee that he had paid court to the dead girl by climbing through her bedroom window at night, and that he had buried the baby in a shoebox.

The grave had been shallow, and was discovered by dogs and dug up. Young boys had taken the body from the dogs and were playing games with it. The entire town was horrified at the occurrence and the sordid tale.

Fee had advised the young man to get out of town and the country if he valued his neck and he took the advice. After confessing to the coroner's jury his part in the escape of the of the seducer, Larry Fee said he was sorry and he didn't know why he had given such advice. He still was elected as the town peace-keeper alternately with Colford, with only two or three exceptions. It seemed almost a custom to have the job passed between John Colford and Lawrence Fee every few years.

When Colford lost to Fee after his street crew of tramps sneaked away, he leased Joe Brammer's "Old Stand" and became a saloonkeeper for the next few years. Later, of course, the incident of tramps was forgotten or forgiven, and Colford once again wore a star.

Lawrence Fee was Deputy when the incident

involving Watkins arose. Jack Watkins, frequently referred to as Wadkins, was said to be polite, kind and a rare gentleman when he was sober. A few drinks changed his complexion remarkably. He hung out part of the time around Lookout, a railroad siding west of Laramie, and came to town periodically on business or to relieve a thirst.

On this occasion Watkins and a friend named Rogers went to the courthouse on business. Sheriff Brophy wanted Rogers on some minor charge and he and Deputy Fee tried to serve the man with a warrant and arrest him. This didn't set too well with Watkins and he pulled a gun. In the exchange of lead, one of his bullets "struck Fee in the leg and another creased the Sheriff's belly." Rogers and Watkins fled for the eastern hills.

The Sheriff speedily recovered. Fee refused to have the lead removed so limped around for a number of years—possibly partly to keep the incident and his bravery fresh in the minds of the townspeople. When he at last consented to the removal, he wore the pellet prominently displayed as a watch fob.

Sheriff Brophy swore out a flyer on the miscreants. He described Watkins as "6 feet tall. About 35. Blue eyes, light brown hair, a very light moustache. Eyelashes entirely wanting. Wanted for murderous assault on Sheriff and Deputy. Shooting and wounding."

Watkins and friend had disappeared. Some months later news from Rawlins informed Laramie authorities that Watkins was in jail there and couldn't pay his fine. Did Laramie want him badly enough to pay the expense of transportation? Laramie didn't. Watkins laid out his sentence and fine at Carbon County's expense.

This involvement of Fee with the Watkins incident was a deciding factor in the frequent turnover in elections between Fee and Colford. As peacekeepers, neither seemed to be prize-winners.

Neither Colford nor Fee had ever seemed to find

the dives, gaming rooms and/or brothels detrimental to the city. Both made their frequent calls, collected fines from madams and pimps alike, and no report of iniquitous activities ever came from them.

It was during one of Colford's "terms" in 1887 that he and Hayford tangled. The frequency of his tenure evidently gave Colford the idea that he could do no wrong. The epitome of the swaggering frontier bully-cop, was Colford.

There had been complaints, off and on, about laxity among elected officials, and Hayford had published some of the complaints. Colford accused him of spiteful and hate-filled remarks among other things. Hayford replied in the columns of the *Sentinel*:

> The City Marshall is respectfully informed that the Sentinel is not run to spite anybody. He is elected to serve the people and not to rule over them. If he will stop his boyish foolishness (Colford was about 50 at that time) and quit loafing in the grogshops and quit his gambling and card playing and attend to his duties enforcing the law, preserving order and making vice and crime take a back seat instead of flaunting himself in the faces of respectable people, no one will give him more encouragement and moral support than we. If he doesn't do this we will agree to make life a burden for all the years to come ... he is the servant of the people as much as if he were a hired girl ...

Perhaps it was the comparison to a hired girl that provoked the wrath of Colford. In a strongly worded letter he turned in his resignation. There was talk of appointing Fee to the post, but since there was little difference between their official performances this was not done. John Sharp was named as replacement instead.

For a time, then, the town seemed a bit quieter and more orderly.

Eight

The Hayford-Gates newspaper had been the only voice for the Gem City from May 1, 1869 until December, 1871. On that date E. A. Slack and T. J. Webster began publication of a six- column daily which they called the *Laramie Daily Independent.*

The *Daily Sentinel* "supported the Territorial administration of Governor J. H. Thayer and was generally republican minded, strongly advocating the best interests and growth of people and the territory," according to J. H. Triggs' summary of the Laramie newspapers in his *City Directory* of 1875, and, he continued:

The *Daily Independent* began publishing,

> with a strong opposition to the Territorial Administration. Although claiming to be independent in politics . . . this paper espoused the cause of the Liberal Republicans in 1872 and hoisted the name of Horace Greeley, and consequently drew a good support from (that party) . . . and the Democrat party . . . .

And then, on March 1, 1875, Charles W. Bramel, Esq., able attorney, bought the newspaper interests of T. J. Webster. Bramel and Slack continued publishing the *Independent* on Second Street across from the Frontier Hotel. They later changed the title of the paper to the *Laramie Daily Chronicle* (sometimes referred to as The Kronk by other papers) and moved to upstairs rooms in Ivinson's bank building. Triggs further states that the *Chronicle* "espoused the cause of the Democratic Party in its most unterrified form." And then it was that Bramel felt the full force of Hayford's teaspoon . . . .

In all these years while the townspeople struggled

to establish Laramie City as a town where the finest people would be happy to make their home and fortune, the ladies of Laramie were neither idle nor neglectful.

The daily routine of cooking, sewing (often by hand) for their families, washing their clothes, using scrub-board and galvanized tub and homemade lye soap, dosing chills and ills of family members kept the Laramie homemaker busy from pre- dawn to late night. Next to these primary necessities came concern for the education and spiritual welfare of the family.

In the summer of 1868, Triggs relates, Mrs. Charles Wright, her daughter Jennie Wright Lancaster and Jane Ivinson set about organizing some sort of formal instruction for the youngsters in town. They first set up Sunday School classes, and before long the formal 3Rs were made available. Enthusiasm was always high in the Gem City and soon there were five churches and two church-affiliated schools ministering to the spiritual and secular life of the community.

The first church to appear in Laramie was the Episcopal, built at the corner of Third and South A and completed in September, 1869. The Methodist Episcopal, completed in December, 1870, stood at the corner of Centre and Second. The Roman Catholic, at Fourth and South B, was started in May, 1869 but experienced money problems and was not completed until the fall of 1871. Until the church was finished, M. H. Murphy opened his home above the saloon for services. A merchant or two made an empty store room available to Protestants until suitable housing was ready. When one church was completed, its doors were opened to other denominations.

These three churches were designed by Laramie architect James Adams and followed the clean, simple lines of churches found in New England communities. The spartan design with the upward-reaching steeple or bell-tower evoked a sense of tranquility, inspiration and comfort, and a feeling of 'back home.'

In January, 1870, the Baptist Church was organized. Their building, completed the same year, also was used as a school. It was known as the Wyoming Institute and served the community well. Director was the Reverend D. J. Pierce, "foremost in organization of nearly all our institutions for intelligence and morality." Mrs. Pierce served as Preceptress.

Somehow the idea grew that the school was only for those of Baptist persuasion so that much of its good service was lost and this also created a financial problem. A number of pupils from Fort Sanders attended regularly, which helped alleviate that embarrassment.

The other church-school, St. Mary's Seminary, came later. This facility stood on north Third and Centre. Farther north, at Third and Fremont, the Presbyterians erected their building in 1871.

This cluster of churches within a three block area was immediately named 'Piety Hill' by the ubiquitous frontier wag. In later years when newer, larger churches were raised along Grand Avenue (B) and blocks on either side, that, too, was called Piety Hill. A Cheyenne newspaper of that early day informed the world that Laramie City did, indeed, have a Piety Hill and it included a saloon, too.

Besides these organized religious sects, J. H. Triggs informs in his *1875 Directory* that there was a "large number of good citizens who are Free-Thinkers, but without any organization, who are ever ready to unite with good people of all creeds and beliefs in every project calculated to benefit mankind."

Too often the pioneers are thought to be ignorant, with a low grade style of speech and lower level of conduct. But there is always a brighter side to the picture.

Formal instruction of the day was strict and had

remarkable staying power. Most emigrants were well-read and they brought with them their books and papers and magazines which they were pleased to share. In 1870 the Wyoming Library and Literary Association was organized to feed the inquiring minds of the city. A collection of one thousand books was first housed in Dr. Finfrock's office on South A Street. In addition to the literary collection for awakening the intelligence of the town, there arose the Laramie Minstrel Troupe to add entertainment for those not given to visiting Front Street's gardens of the night. After the closing of the old National Theatre on First Street, traveling Thespians and vaudeville acts performed in Ivinson's Hall on Second Street or in another building pompously advertised as the "Best Opera House in Town."

One of the offerings of the Laramie Minstrel Troupe was roundly criticized in the *Sentinel* by the Reverend Pierce of the Baptist Institute as "vulgar and lacking in taste." This chastisement was rather warmly answered in the newspaper the following day by the play's director. The wordy exchange brought immediate results. Attendance at the next performance was greatly increased.

Triggs' *City Directory* mentions the fraternal organizations which held a prominent place in the social life for the men of the town. There was no mention, however, of the negro lodge which was only referred to in the newspaper as the Negro Hall. Nor was a location given. There was an item, however, which repeated the notice posted on the lodge door: "No gentleman admitted unless he comes himself."

Triggs' comments on the organizations in Laramie adds a three-line note on "Sons of Temperance," which was organized in January of 1875. This was followed a few months later by the Murphy Temperance Union (no connection there with Mike Murphy's Saloon on Front Street).

This early introduction of a temperance movement in Laramie found a host of willing workers in town. There were many men favorably inclined toward temperance. The women, too, through first-hand experience with family problems created by strong drink, were diligent and almost unanimously supporters.

Continuous efforts were made to require all dispensaries to close on the Sabbath. Laramie was successful for only brief periods, but never permanently in those early turbulent years.

The *Sentinel* voiced the general relief and pleasure of the town for one brief respite. In a fairly lengthy article printed on a fine June Monday:

> Yesterday was the quietest Sunday on our streets that we have experienced. There was no drunkenness except one or two . . . soldiers (who) came into town already primed. Everybody felt free to pass up and down the principal streets without fear of insult or annoyance.

The keepers of the grogshops were praised for complying with the law. The next week, however, the tune was in a different key.

Hayford, as the voice of the Plains, had promoted the Temperance movement from its beginnings. His sharp criticisms and praise (when due) of grogsellers kept public feathers ruffled or smoothed according to his printed word.

Immediately after the quiet, pleasurable Sunday several purveyors of ardent spirits stopped their subscriptions to the *Sentinel*. This was the lowest of blows to Hayford, for his rates were already at give-away point. He depended on job-printing to pay his help and keep his own family fed and clad. At one point he stated that a first rate newspaper needed no less than $175 per week to keep on top of the red ink. He didn't always make that. He constantly printed his thanks to various townspeople for gratuities in the form of fish, vegetables from home gardens, freshly butchered meat and fresh ranch butter or eggs.

To supplement his income, also adding personal prestige as a willing public servant (if he needed that), he fulfilled a number of public offices at various times. These paid regular wages, of course, but none large enough to excite envy. He served as Judge (he had passed the bar exams in several states), as Postmaster, a much sought appointment; he served as Territorial Auditor, as County Superintendent of Schools, and in various elective county offices.

Money wasn't the only concern, however. The cancellations were just as great a blow to his editorial pride as to his purse. These men "were willing to do without the *Sentinel* !"

So when his carrier boy reported the cancellations the Editor printed his testy response:

> John, carrier boy for the Sentinel, wears the Temperance Union Badge and the Blue Ribbon. Now this is costing the Sentinel money and we propose to discharge every one of these temperance employees and fill their places with men who will spend a good deal of time and all of their money in the dram shops. Selah.

And he proceeded to tick off the rebels by name. They were Johannes Gerber and Fred Bath of the Tivoli, Fred Hesse, H. Shroyer, Joe Brammer (who constantly ran afoul of the law and later moved out by Sunnyside), M. Madsen and a carpenter named B. F. Smith (the wife-beater). They had, he reported, all stopped their paper because it "gave a mild sort of assent to the temperance reform and because John wore the Blue Ribbon. These men believe in intemperance (and) are willing to 'do without the *Sentinel*' rather than encourage and patronize a newspaper (that backs) the temperance movement."

Then he added a scathing indictment of the man who tried the editorial patience sorely:

There is one other man, too, J. Fein, who took the *Sentinel* as long as the boy would carry it to him for he conscientiously refused to pay for it. (His) reason is that it is opposed to gambling houses, houses of prostitution, keeping liquor houses open on the Sabbath, etc. So Jake also is consistent in his principles.

The subscriptions were eventually renewed. Even Fein paid up.

Bill Nye, of course, was working on the *Sentinel* at that time. He might have composed the foregoing except for the well-known-about-town fact that the edge of the Nye thirst ran extra deep, and his capacity was smaller than his thirst.

Nye was highly popular in town, another fact that sometimes grated on the Hayford nerves. Hostesses sought out the young man for the liveliness and humor he added to any gathering. But after he had ruined more than one carpet, the ladies pursued a practice designed to keep him from too close attendance on the punchbowl. An audience of attentive, attractive young women kept the Nye wit in top-form. He enjoyed himself, the guests enjoyed him, carpets were safe and the party's success well assured. After Nye was married, his thirst was less apparent.

An interesting invitation was tendered to Bill Nye by the Laramie Temperance Union to speak on the subject at the weekly meeting of the Guild. At first Nye refused the bid but later agreed. A newspaper report of the meeting and lecture related that Nye rambled on for twenty to thirty minutes, reminding the audience that men of far more drinking experience than he had already covered the ground. "It is not the besotted rum-guzzler who does the damage to society," he stated, "but the high-toned young men and youths."

After talking for a half-hour or more Nye apologized for not being prepared to give a speech.

Liquor was always of paramount interest in

Laramie, no matter the times. Many years later it still occupied a large part of life in the town. One concerned citizen might be forgiven for calling out the Laramie Fire Department to investigate some barrels containing an unknown liquid which was finally found to be water.

Even though Hayford was fond of bragging that Laramie was the livest town on the entire U. P. line, a reporter for *Leslie's Weekly*, on tour across the nation, looked upon the little town sprawled on the dry western plain and condemned it.

" . . . as seen from the train Laramie City is not half hard enough to please our exigent seekers after excitement and novelty . . . ."

Had that effete Easterner dared get off that train he would have quickly learned how deep were the waters that seemed to run so quietly.

Nine

Wyoming Territory surprised the world in December, 1869, by recognizing women as human beings with ability to think and reason (although some men believed they should do so only as directed), and passed a law that allowed women to vote, hold office and "own property in their own name and to enjoy the fruits of their labors."

No different from the men, then, sometimes ladies found a distinct preference for the same bit of land. And when they had the money they went after it, just as the men did. So disputes arose on the distaff side, too. One such occasion was briefly mentioned as a "squaw fight" between two women who claimed the same lot. There was a spate of words, a scuffle, a tussle and some hair pulling. The reporter must have left very quietly from the scene for he never did tell the outcome.

City lots in the downtown district were 24 feet wide by 132 feet from street to alley. In the beginning, many strips were sold by metes and bounds or, when a building overlapped a lot line, it was described as an "irregular" tract. Thus buildings weren't always "square" with the world and might face onto street or alley and still do a good business. There were also numerous dwellings facing onto alleys well into the 20th century.

Such vagaries caused much friction. One such cause was a plot on Third Street, measuring 8 feet deep with a 48 foot frontage. The argument led to blows and some red blood, this time between men. The argument was finally settled for $200. Women had little cash to their names so couldn't settle arguments in such "gentlemanly" fashion.

Then, the spring court term opened in March 1870, and the world was startled anew to learn that women were allowed to serve on al trial jury in Laramie.

This panel, composed of six women and six men, heard testimony in trials for horse and cattle thieves, for illegal branding as well as a case of murder. The court session was held in Trabing's old Blue Front building on rowdy First Street. Chief Justice John H. Howe, described as "peevish and fretful, with a dyspeptic stomach, but a man of good ability" presided at this historic court session.

Because of the rash of coarse jokes and expressed disbelief in their mental abilities, the women were hesitant to serve on the jury. The Judge, however, assured the women that there was "not the slightest impropriety in any lady occupying the position" on the jury.

One of the abiding good results of having women jurors was that drinking, smoking and card and dice playing was discontinued during court sessions. Men no longer loosened their ties or discarded their coats, and they kept their feet off the empty chairs nearby, even the judge kept his feet on the floor instead of across his desk-corner. And spitting was confined to the many spittoons in the courtroom.

That famous mixed jury brought congratulations from many world figures and heads of state. At the end of the long, tedious term of court it was generally conceded that the law had been enforced and "equal, impartial, exact justice meted out to all in every instance" and that the women had "acquitted themselves with dignity and rendered verdicts befitting the occasion," thus confounding numbers of skeptical chin-pullers.

Of all the cases heard, the murder occasioned the most interest. The event had occurred in the Shamrock Hotel when a rounder and sure-shot named John Hoctor was "taming" the barroom. A couple of his wild shots penetrated the floor of an upstairs bedroom where Andrew Howie, a bullwhacker lately in from the trail, was trying to get some sleep.

Since the shots narrowly missed him, Howie was disturbed and got dressed and went downstairs, gun in hand, to see what was going on.

Hoctor still had the barroom treed when Howie stepped through the door and was immediately confronted by Hoctor. The drunken gunman bawled out "I'm going to shoot you," and he and Howie fired simultaneously. At the same time there were other shots and the lights went out.

When the kerosene lamps were again lit it was seen that Hoctor was dead and Patrick Doran had been hit.

"Pat! You're hurt!" a friend exclaimed.

"No, I guess not," the Irishman replied and got up from the floor dripping blood.

A bullet had hit Doran in the upper arm. He was pretty shaky for a time, but with the lead removed, a good bandage applied and a stiff drink under his belt, the tall, lean Irishman was again on his feet tending bar.

Howie surrendered to Albany County Sheriff N. K. Boswell, along with a few others who had fired shots, and they were confined in the guardhouse at Fort Sanders. Howie admitted that he had probably been the one who killed Hoctor.

Since Howie was a tall young man, blue-eyed, and of handsome and appealing countenance, bets were laid that the ladies of the jury would all vote for acquittal. There was general surprise when the verdict was "guilty of manslaughter in the first degree." The sentence: ten years at hard labor in the Detroit (Michigan) House of Correction. (At this time it was where Territorial prisoners were sent. The Penitentiary was not built until 1872.) Some indignation was voiced: what about self-defense? Two years later the young man was pardoned and all trace of him apparently lost.

In April, 1871, women again served on a jury, again in the Blue Front grogshop, and for a third time in September of the same year. But the September session met in a more appropriate place, in rooms on the second floor of Wagner's store. Thereafter Court was held in the new courthouse which was ready for use early in 1872.

Between these two court terms an interesting letter about the women jurors appeared in the *Daily Sentinel*, written by M. M. (Brick) Pomeroy "a writer of eminence."

His opening remarks were complimentary to Laramie, and the fact that this little frontier town on the edge of the world had allowed women to move to a position beside the menfolk, then this letter continued:

> ... up to the time the right of suffrage had been given to women in Laramie there had been a few houses of prostitution, relics left by the railroad pioneers for the edification of those who might come after them ... the duty of this grand jury (was) to examine into the habits, customs, "morals" peculiarities and iniquities of the ones charged with offending the peace and morality of Laramie, so this jury went to work.
>
> The women visited not only the saloons, but they went from one place of prostitution to another to see for themselves. They talked with the female inmates, inquiring into their mode and manner of life, the profits of the business, they learned the names of their patrons and frequency of visits ...
>
> The women of easy virtue replied frankly and asked only to be fairly dealt with. They claimed, with some degree of truth, that it was no worse for them to live in such houses than for the husbands of the women visitors to patronize them.
>
> They do say that when the women jurors returned to their homes after that grand tour of inspection, more than one of them told her husband she had a little something to say to him in the bedroom out of earshot of the children.

Some very red-eared men sputtered and stammered: 'Oh! Pshaw! now, don't — don't you believe such stories.'

'Oh! but well, you know how it is — ,' the wife replied.

Supper in some homes was a silent meal. After supper the jury-women met to consult with themselves. The husbands went out to meet in little groups here and there, on street corners, behind some store, under some shed, or behind a train of cars. Consultation over, the women returned to their homes, while toward the wee sma' hours, we are told, the husbands came in, silent and thoughtful.

When the morning sun arose the Cyprians, like the Arabs, had folded their tents and silently stole away . . .

. . . The people of Laramie seem to have forgotten to quarrel and bicker and back-bite among themselves . . . From all we learn, Laramie is one of the most mellow-hearted, brotherly, christianized places on the American continent.

This splendid picture of domestic bliss was "drawn largely on imagination," so the newspaper editor stated. If it had been dated several years later it might have been laid to Bill Nye's pen, but there evidently was a "writer of eminence" named Pomeroy in Laramie at that time. He was a mining engineer from the east out looking over prospective mining sites with a group of four other men. In 1875 the Sentinel stated that "Brick Pomeroy lay dangerously ill at his residence in New York." No other details were found.

As to the elaborate tale: In the first place no jury was empaneled to serve other than during the legal court term.

In the second place, the Cyprians' tents all remained in place and only a week after the eminent writer's letter appeared in print a "house of ill-shape" was brought to public attention.

This unshapely house was "so far off and kept so quiet few even knew or paid attention to it" (which may explain how it was "missed by the ladies of the jury"), "but," the *Sentinel* rambled on, certainly assuring

Laramie's male population that all was not lost. "one night there was more noise than usual. So much boisterous hilarity and loud noise was there that it attracted the attention of the watchful guardians of the public peace."

Kate Boyd, the "head devil of the place" was arrested and brought before Esquire Pease to receive a lecture and a fine of $25.

The despairing notation was added "We understand the parties now have left town."

But there was no cause for despair. Laramie still had Madam Fay. And Pawnee Liz and Emma Christy. And Julia Coyle and Nettie (Nellie) Wright among others.

It was Liz and Emma who rented a driving rig from Ingersoll's stables and set out "in a hilarious state for a ride." Near the depot their horse took fright and made a short, tight turn, upsetting the buggy and spilling the two frail sisters. One fell upon the other, they bumped heads painfully, and the buggy whacked them both good and hard. The horse dashed away dragging the rig and was finally stopped at the Rolling Mill Hotel. The horse was unharmed but the buggy was "used up almost completely."

Friends took the two women home and called a doctor. Their wounds were treated and it was reported the two were doing well and able to receive visitors.

A wicked man named James Wilson was taken to court soon afterward by Pawnee Liz and accused of "removing $160 from her Bible where it had been hidden."

Wilson admitted he had spent the night in the house, but denied taking the lady's hard-earned money. He was tried, found not guilty, but fined $5 anyway and released.

Lizzie Stevens (Pawnee Liz) and Julia Coyle, a young girl "managed by Liz," appeared regularly on charges of prostitution. They were slapped on the wrist, lectured, fined and released just as regularly.

There was much gossip and horrified clucking among townspeople over these pleasure houses, and the Sentinel repeatedly stated that the "intention of the authorities was to make life so miserable for them (the prostitutes) they will pack up their tents and steal away."

But their tents remained in place. After all Pawnee Liz conducted a legitimate business as laundress for a cafe and hotel, she owned her own home at Third and South C (Garfield), and if she had a hobby or sideline —

On complaint of a neighbor Liz and Julia Coyle were hauled into court along with one Mr. Connell. Complainant was A. J. House, a guard at the penitentiary. Specifics of the complaint were not made public but House may have been losing sleep listening in on the revelry next door.

Judge Donnellan levied the usual $7 fine plus costs, administering the usual lecture and the "girls" were free to go. Nowhere was Connell mentioned. (The $7 fine depended on the presiding judge. It was said that that was the limit set by law.)

If the authorities really meant to make life miserable for les filles des joies their approach was quite gentle. It may have been because too many "respectable" men were involved and not enough evidence could be drawn to convict on grounds of "public nuisance" or other.

The newspaper report added that the arrests of Liz and Julia were made at the Stevens home and not at Sunnyside. At this time, also, it was noted that the Sunnyside "resort" was outside the city limits, therefore the city had no jurisdiction.

The Sunnyside was one of Laramie's houses of "known reputation," and apparently had not been a part of the "tour of inspection" conducted by the women-jurors.

Located at the southern end of Second Street, in the old "tin-town" of pre-railroad days and since absorbed by the activities of Laramie City, the Sunnyside dance-hall lasted well into the 1920's as a resort of great attraction. Later it sported a coat of gleaming white paint, a renovation to the interior and became a respectable dwelling for a respectable family. But in the beginning it was a part of the homestead of James A. Sherrod.

In a twentieth century column of reminiscences of early days in Laramie, W. E. Chaplin, newspaperman, related that the resort belonged to Sherrod. That pioneer, who at age 30 was affectionately called "Old Sherrod", neither drank nor smoked, and did not frequent the tavern. But his wife, a Cherokee woman, did enjoy the happy-go-lucky atmosphere of the place. She and the Sherrod daughters, Chaplin related, dressed in gaudy clothes and whiled away the time that Sherrod was on the road as government scout, or mail carrier to the Hahn's Peak area, or guide for miners and hunters in the mountains. Chaplin at no time suggested that Mrs. Sherrod or the girls joined in the shenanigans at Sunnyside, nor did he ever mention it was a "house of mistaken-use."

A year after the incident with Liz, Julia, and House, the newspapers noted that the Sunnyside was "rising into notice again" and was turning out the usual numbers of black eyes and mansard roofs on Saturday nights." A follow-up item noted that fifty-seven soldiers were in the guardhouse as a result of pay day and putting a bit too much money into concentrated joy.

The next day's paper posted a notice of a general court martial in session at Fort Sanders "which will be convened for several days."

On isolated occasions men who kept a "common, ill-governed and disorderly house" were called before the court. A change of venue was frequently granted them, which undoubtedly assured a sympathetic judge. Back in those good ole days, just as in the present, the court too often "found" for the fullest purse.

One of Laramie's businessmen owned a number of houses, two of which were located at South D (Custer) and Third. He rented one of the properties to two seamstresses, "women of impeccable reputation," and the other to a "weak sister of the Magdalene persuasion" who kept a house in a disorderly manner.

On complaint of the sewing ladies, the frail sister was arrested and was to have a jury trial. She made several thoughtful suggestions as to jurors, mentioning two certain merchants on Second Street who would make good jurors.

Editor Hayford, with tongue in tobacco-cheek, slyly suggested that the men "must have buildings to let to be so chosen, for both were married men."

Selection of jurors proceeded according to form. The defendant objected to a certain juror because "he had become very angry when she refused to let him and another man rent a room in her 'boarding house' without cash in advance." She did not challenge the man who was with him.

The trial proceeded in order. The Court (Judge N. L. Andrews, well-known wag and prankster) at last informed the defendant that she could examine "the witness."

"The Magdalene turned and glared at the witness and lit into her. The way those two women went at it was a terror," the news reporter reported solemnly. "At last the Court had to interpose."

The jury found the defendant guilty to the extent of $15 plus costs which she promptly paid. Her companion plead guilty, received the usual "severe lecture', was fined $2 plus costs and let off.

The "fallen women" sometimes went visiting friends in other places in other towns. Not always with the happiest of results.

When Emma Christy went to Cheyenne to visit, she met a bartender and fell in love with him. The bartender felt he was on a higher social plane than Emma and did not return her affection. The Laramie newspaper reported with apparent surprise that Emma had killed herself for love.

Her story seemed to follow the usual pattern: Daughter of a "fine, wealthy family" from back east. Her family had disapproved of her decision to marry Henry Christie (Christy). They had eloped. A few weeks later, with no family money coming to Emma, Henry deserted her. She couldn't go home, of course. She went to Denver for a year, drifted to other frontier towns, then came to Laramie.

The Rev. F. W. Thompson of Cheyenne's Episcopal Church "made a few appropriate remarks at the burial of the suicide."

Comment in the *Sentinel* was different: "Love springs immortal from the breast of woman, no matter how low she may have sunk in the pool of turpitude."

Without doubt, when the news reached the "boarding houses" in Laramie, many a girl wept for Emma and her unrequited love. Probably some of the tears were for themselves as well. After all, was there any love or hope of love for any of them?

And when May Howard came over the hill from Cheyenne and was accidentally shot and killed in Nellie Wright's Front Street bordello, called by courtesy of the press "The Crystal Wine Parlors," there was hardly a stir. Texas Jim (no other name given) who shot the girl, was "honorably acquitted."

Killing a prostitute was not a hanging offense.

Onto this scene, then, in August 1875, stepped the new pastor of the Methodist Episcopal Church, the Reverend J. A. Edmondson.

Ten

From the wooded hills of Tennessee came a tall, bony preacher who "leaned into the day." A man of great earnestness and dedication. It is impossible to know what challenges he expected and hoped to overcome, or how much he hoped to accomplish for the good of the people of Laramie.

The church of his parish was found at the corner of Second Street and Centre. It was a small frame building barely six years old, once painted a ghastly yellow which the years and harsh winters had worn to a fair cream color. The open cupola stood empty of a bell. The new minister learned quickly to compete with the booming city fire-bell on the neighboring lot.

Stakes and markings outlined the location of the future parsonage. Much of the man's frustrations and anxieties undoubtedly were vented right there during his tenure in Laramie because the Reverend J. A. Edmondson built much of that one-room house himself. Later Charles Klingerman was hired to add a second room. But in the beginning, the new pastor would have been hopeful, full of pleasure and zeal for his faith's endeavor.

Membership in the Methodist Episcopal Church was still small in 1875, no more than three dozen, and due to the practice of the Methodist Conference in changing pastors every year, or two at the most, much had to be accomplished in a short time.

If the Tennessee hill-man was eager to learn something of his new environment he hadn't long to wait. The town showed him the water and shoved him in for baptism.

If he had no previous inkling of the numerous parlor houses and fig-leaf culture of the city they were brought sharply to his attention by the suicide of a First Street 'boarder' named Dora Marr. Nor could the regular arrests and fines of the ladies of the night scarcely have gone unnoticed.

The very day of his arrival William S. Fowler was being tried for assault and attempted murder of Mike O'Brien. O'Brien, recently released from the Territorial Penitentiary, had gone to a disreputable house out toward Fort Sanders known as the Double Decker. Fowler was already there and wouldn't let O'Brien in. They argued. They tangled. Fowler broke the O'Brien arm and "used him up quite badly." For this impertinence Fowler was faced with a prison term of one year and a fine not to exceed $1,000 to be fixed by the court. What the Court did was fine him $100 and sent him up for six months to think over his bad temper.

On this same day another newcomer caught the public's attention. The new Warden of the Territorial Penitentiary, a Major Wood, came to town.

The Cheyenne Leader published an effusive introduction of the gentleman: "Major Wood . . . highly recommended by his former employers, the officers of the Baltimore and Ohio Railway Company . . . He had been with them for twelve years at Harper's Ferry and four years prior to that the Major had served as Assistant Warden in the State Prison at Clinton, New York where he had charge over 1200 convicts . . . his knowledge and experience promises prudence and economy . . ." in the conduct of the Wyoming facility.

Wood came and saw and left.

He liked nothing about the Penitentiary, the town, or the broad, silent plains, frightening in their haunting beauty. He took the first train east.

The town went into a tailspin at being so rudely spurned by a dude from back east. The hubbub didn't last long, though, there were too many things going on, and the new preacher to initiate.

Since there were already four clergymen ministering to the spiritual needs of the Gem City, the advent of one more could hardly be expected to cause much of a ripple in the town's whirlpool.

And after rumors and repercussions of the Marr and Fowler affairs, Edmondson probably revised whatever opinions he may have had concerning the twenty-five grogshops and other pleasure establishments which were not always conducted in the most refined manner.

By the end of his first six months in Laramie, the Reverend Mr. Edmondson was pretty well informed on the goings-on about town. And he learned further the practices of some elected officials when George Ritter took his Christmas vacation on County funds.

Then there was always the problem of tramps and down-and-outers. Without doubt, many of these travelers stopped off at private homes in town for a bit of charity. The city did, however, periodically round up some of the hoboes from their hang-outs in alley shacks and sheds or at the beer garden, or wherever they could be found. When vagrants and hoboes were arrested, they were often put to work on the city streets. When one work-gang asked for time to find additional tools and failed to return, the city fathers ordered Marshall John Colford to cut short his card game and keep at least one eye on his charges.

Some vagrants aroused the compassion of Laramie's people. A father and his 7-year old son, discovered lying close together on the ground at the Birnie stone works, were found to be destitute, insufficiently clothed for Laramie's winter weather, and near starvation. They were commended to the charity of the city.

Another man in need was found sleeping on the steps of the Methodist Church. This church was the nearest to the railroad yards and since most such wanderers rode the rails it is not surprising that they should apply at the church for help. And the Reverend Edmondson was ready to help anyone in need, as were others of compassion in town. Rowdy and wayward as Laramie City was, it was not stingy. Ministers were often called to give counselling, comfort and solace when knights of the bar met in combat. Only a block from Edmondson's church, in Robinson's saloon, occurred a bloody fight. John Hussy and Davy Jones (his real name) went after each other with pocket-knives. Their argument was over a 50 cent bet. Both were handy with the blade and both were badly cut up. Jones called for a doctor and a preacher and Hussy called for fine-money and a lawyer.

Some of the saloon keepers regularly closed their places on Sundays and herded their barflies to church. Such was Tom Dayton when he kept bar at the northwest corner of South A and First Street. He and his patrons had regular pews reserved for them at the Methodist Church and their singing was wonderful inspiration, according to memoirs left by Martha Wallis.

Jack Connors was another. Connors twice invited Edmondson to preach in his saloon, the Wyoming Billiard Hall, one block south of the Methodist Church.

Western tales put the circuit rider or western preacher in the saloon wearing the full armament of the frontiersman. Edmondson wore the full armor of his faith in God with the Bible as his side-arm.

There is no public record of the sermons he delivered in the Wyoming Billiard Hall, nor is there any record of what effect his works may have had on the audience. It must have had some effect on the saloonkeeper himself for when Connors was later re-elected to the Mayor slot he strongly advocated the closing of all saloons and gaming rooms on Sundays.

This touched off a fuse among the grogsellers and innkeepers who up to that time were ninety-nine and a half percent German with the other fraction of a percent Irish.

The resulting uproar brought forth these facetious lines in the newspaper: "Donner und Blitzen! Mein Gott in Himmell! Three more years of Jack Connor! How can we stand it!"

All ministers were in agreement on the Sunday closings. But as usual, Edmondson, being the most outspoken, presented the nearest target for blame.

This tall, bony man who leaned into the wind was a strong and forceful speaker, unafraid of argument and dissent. Indeed, it appears that he may have sought dissention by the topics he selected for his sermons.

In May of 1876, Charles W. Bramel, the wordy lawyer who frequently crossed verbal swords with Hayford, had become owner of a newspaper. He had named the sheet the Daily Chronicle and set out to outdo Hayford as a wordsmith. Bramel was a member of the Methodist Church and it was not long before he locked horns with his pastor over scriptural interpretation. He used his newspaper columns as a public forum.

Much of the feud carried on by these two southerners was verbal, so those portions appearing in print leave much of the by-play to the imagination. A large part of their feud also had to do with the Civil War which, although the shooting had ended ten years past, continued to be fought for the next half-century.

Even though these two men were southerners, their disagreement came about partly because Edmondson, whose parents had been slave-holders, strongly proclaimed his lifelong advocacy of "Better to abolish slavery than to destroy the Union."

Perhaps Bramel really agreed, but was contrary enough to take the opposite view. There were many pro-slavery people in Laramie, Bramel's close friends.

Some of them, like Bramel, were from Missouri where the question had been bitterly fought.

Edmondson was described as being a bold, outspoken man with an abrasive manner. Bramel was the same. Little wonder they disagreed.

Bramel apparently re-preached a few of Edmondson's sermons in his paper, and the pastor must as surely have resented it. And if it wasn't a re-preachment, then Bramel surely tried to advise the cleric what he should and should not talk about.

Copies of the Chronicle containing much of this exchange are not available, hence the numerous quotes from the Daily and Weekly Sentinel.

The Chronicle for September 4 "contained a sort of threat, and partly a caution to a certain minister to be careful and not meddle with politics. This remark," as explained in the Sentinel had its origin "in a conversation wherein the Rev. Edmondson, in the presence of the editor of the Chronicle, expressed the idea that it was the duty of the city authorities to enforce the law requiring the closing of business houses and saloons on the Sabbath."

The editor of the Chronicle replied that "were the city authorities to do this, they never could be re-elected!" Bramel, the writer continued, thought a minister of the gospel must say nothing about politics, it was not his provenance and he had better be careful what he said, in the pulpit and out.

The *Sentinel* explained at length how it should be a minister's concern to preach and teach against sin wherever it may be found.

> And when it comes to that, men who, for the sake of gratifying their own personal ambition, or for the sake of success of their political party, will openly advocate the violation of the law of the land and disregard the law of God, it is time that watchmen on the walls of Zion should lift up their voices in warning . . .

> ... if temperance and observance of the Sabbath are not proper subjects for the ministers to advocate, then their sphere of duty must be very circumscribed indeed, and we are glad that at least one of them had the moral courage to come out plainly on the questions in spite of the covert threats ...

Edmondson declared he would discuss those who broke the laws in Laramie, and those who allowed it to continue, despite a "threat to assassinate" him, and added "Transgressors are permitted to come up before the powers that be and pay $2 per month for the privilege of violating the law ... It is said parties are allowed to come up and pay $50 for a certain length of time for the privilege of violating any law that might conflict with their business. A business that can only exist by a violation of the law." This, of course, brought repercussions from many sides.

From many of the remarks printed in the Sentinel, it appeared to be a wide-held idea that Bramel, in publishing his news-sheet was using it only as a public forum to expound his views, and the views of his political party. Hayford constantly referred to the sheet as the party's organ.

In February, 1875, the City had passed an ordinance against all kinds of gambling. The law was only symbolically enforced, as was a ruling against bars and drinking establishments selling their products on Sundays. So there was another bone to be chewed on.

In late September the *Sentinel* ran the following paragraphs from the Reverend Edmondson:

TO THE PUBLIC. LET THE PEOPLE HEAR.

Having been absent on last Sabbath we couldn't continue our sermon on Debauchery of the Public Morals ...

Edmondson then put the following questions to the public:

1. Does public sentiment demand Sabbath desecration in direct violation of the law?

2. Will it tolerate the connivance of officers whose sworn duty it is to enforce the laws and the most open and notorious violations thereof?

Let every law-abiding citizen say to their public servants 'Do your sworn duty.'

And he quoted the Code of Law: Chapter 35, Section 114:

Any guilty of open lewdness or other ... act of public indecency, debauchery of the public morals; who shall keep open gaming houses on the Sabbath day or night, or maintain or keep a lewd house or place for the practice of fornication, or a common, ill-governed and disorderly house ... every such person shall on conviction be fined (to) $100 or imprisonment in the County Jail to six months.

Evidently Bramel printed a hearty response in his newspaper for on the following day Hayford's snappy reply appeared in the *Sentinel's* column in two items:

Quite a sensible well-written article on 'Sabbath Observance' appeared in the Chronicle last evening. We would be glad if the writer favor us with some more of his views and answer a question or two.

Does he believe people should lay aside their ordinary labor and business pursuits on the Sabbath Day and observe it as a day of rest? ... We endorse the Scripture that 'the Sabbath was made for man' and believe the spending of it in that way to get the most real benefit physically, intellectually and morally best pleases the Supreme Being and every man is right to be his own judge in the matter.

And in another column:

We wish to say to the public that the slur in last evening's Chronicle about 'Hayford's efforts to stir up discord,' merely refers to a paid advertisement written and paid for by Mr. Bramel's pastor giving notice of services in Mr. Bramel's church today. (It) is something we had no more to do with than with the Serbian War.

We never passed a word on the subject with Mr. Edmondson, but we have an idea that it is as legitimate as the glowing editorial puffs which appear day to day in Bramel's paper about the variety theatre, or the high-flown tributes to the 'loveliness', 'Beauty' etc. of prostitutes. It is a matter of taste, however, and Mr. Bramel has a right to take his choice.

Words continued to fly, although most of the city's attention was again centered on the normal activities of First Street and environs. Many of those activities bordered on harassment, terrorism and vandalism.

A favorite pastime of young bucks was to congregate on street corners or mid-block and refuse to move if an older person or a woman came along, forcing her to cross the street or if she continued along the boardwalk, they would crowd near and jostle her and make personal remarks.

Another favorite activity of young blades was to make up a gang usually half-hungover, and prowl the town, usually at night, brawling and howling, tearing down signs, piling boxes and barrels before doors, vandalizing property (or stealing it) and "committing nuisances and other disgusting acts in yards and public places."

In one instance the hooligans were rounded up and the two or three among the group "who had no influential friends among the authorities were arrested and fined. The worst six were allowed to go free."

Those fines, by today's standards, were nothing. $4 plus $2.50 costs. But with wages at .30 an hour or one to two dollars for a 10-hour workday, $6.50 was frequently beyond a hoodlum's means. He was then thrown into jail, which often was only a flimsy, slab-sided shack with no caulking in cracks, without heat, often with dirt floor, and no sanitary convenience except a filthy chamber pot for relief.

Such activities disturbed many townsfolk and not only the Rev. Edmondson, but other ministers in town as well as Editor Hayford. Edmondson and Hayford seemed to be the only ones to voice their concern. This they did in their strongest words which brought on another diatribe from Bramel and Reed's *Chronicle*. What the *Chronicle's* exact words were is unknown, but the Sentinel made their meaning clear enough.

"The *Chronicle*," the editor of the *Sentinel* states, "comes out and publishes a threat against a minister of the gospel, in case he dares to say anything in his pulpit against drunkenness and Sabbath breaking and in favor of law and order . . ." and when the preacher does preach on these subjects . . .

> Reed, himself a member of Mr. Edmondson's church and a professed Christian, comes out with a column and a half of low, vile, scurrilous abuse of his pastor — a tirade which would be a disgrace to a bar-room blackguard and . . . (would) disgrace the religion which he professes, injure the church to which he belongs, and destroy the usefulness of the pastor who is his spiritual teacher.
>
> There are plenty of people in any community who are pleased when the cause of religion is ridiculed or damaged, and are tickled to see a row between a minister of the gospel and one of his flock . . . such will laugh . . . and pat Reed on the head . . . but there isn't a person in town who looks at it calmly who doesn't despise him.'

Charlie Bramel accosted the preacher one day in December on Second Street. There was snow on the ground, icy and slushy, and the streets were as usual churned to muck by passing traffic, wheel, horse and human.

The two men were seen to argue and the Rev. Edmondson was heard to shout: "I'm not afraid of you, Bramel!" The next minute he was picking himself up out of the mud and Bramel was walking hurriedly away.

Later, in a store, Bramel made a half- apologetic, half-shamed remark that he had "knocked me down a preacher a bit ago."

This set-to did not end their words. The feud continued until Bramel's *Chronicle* folded three months later. Popular opinion may have had something to do with the paper's demise, for many residents admired the fire-breathing minister. Some even felt that he was too kind to the community.

At Christmas time a number of his admirers gave him a fine, gold-headed cane "to defend himself from Bramel."

In June, Joe H. Brammer had been hauled into court charged with keeping a "house of ill-repute." The usual farce was played: the hearing, the lecture and the fine. This had become so common no one needed a rehearsal and it was these things that kept public indignation at high pitch.

Then in mid-December quite a sensation was created by the arrest and fining of a number of saloonkeepers for not closing their shops on the Sabbath. Several of them reacted loudly and predictably. The same J. H. Brammer was one. No matter that there had been a law passed, it was only loosely enforced, and then in isolated cases.

Brammer was brought to court this time for assault, battery and excessive use of bad language. After four juries had heard the case the verdict was still against him. He appealed again, and the case was carried over to next court-term. Brammer meanwhile moved his business beyond the city limits out near Sunnyside.

A similar charge against L. Abrams found him guilty of using language tending to provoke assault. The verdicts stemmed in part from efforts of all Laramie preachers and the better elements in town, to close the 'dens of vice' on Sundays. Being the most outspoken, Edmondson as usual received most of the blame. When

Charlie Bramel left off chicken-picking with Edmondson another old-timer stepped in. This argument, too, was carried on through the Sentinel's columns. The provoker signed himself "For Good," but everyone in town knew that old wag jokester N. L. Andrews was IT. It wasn't long before their hissing and spitting turned to more serious exchange. Edmondson's habit of announcing his sermon titles in the newspaper gave Andrews, as it had Bramel, chance to compose rebuttal. Two of the earliest, "The Lawless of Laramie" and "The Gambling Hells of Laramie and The Men Who Frequent Them" promised some real fireworks. Edmondson had stated that the persons were all well known, but that he would name names if necessary.

Andrews countered with some personal remarks about the clergyman. He further stated that he didn't think it to the advantage of the city and its good people to bring up its short-comings and failures and expose them to the world. Probably the world would have taken little note had the Bramels and Andrews not called attention to it all.

The words continued to flow as did the liquor across the bars. They became more pointed and personal and N. L. at last overstepped the lines of debate and propriety with insinuations and accusations. Edmondson promptly challenged him to retract his lies or prove them in court of law, or in face-to-face meeting. He didn't accompany his challenge with glove to the Andrews face, but the effect was there.

The subject was dropped, but the damage was done. The matter had gone from entertaining public debate to a smell of scandal.

The Annual Conference of the Methodist Episcopal Church was scheduled for its regular session and everyone was awaiting the outcome. Was the effectiveness of Edmondson's service in Laramie damaged or not? Would he be allowed to remain in Laramie?

There were more supporters of the pastor than might have been supposed. Forty businessmen with other citizens drew up and signed the following petition and sent it to B. F. Cary, Presiding Elder, Northern District of Colorado Conference:

> We, the undersigned, though not members of the Methodist Episcopal Church, but personal friends of J. A. Edmondson, hereby express our confidence in his strict moral integrity, and having witnessed his earnest efforts to build up the best interests of society, most respectfully petition the Conference Board to return said J. A. Edmondson to this charge for another year.

Lengthy debate followed at the Conference. In his annual report to the gathering, the Rev. Dr. Cary used the following language in reference to the work of the Laramie pastor:

> Laramie has been under the pastoral care of the Rev. J. A. Edmondson who has been true to his church and his convictions of right. He has a fearful moral conflict and has stood for reform through all obstacles. He has made his collections by going from person to person and has done a good work in Laramie. He will be remembered by both his friends and enemies.

Twice it was reported that the clergyman would return to Laramie. But the final decision was no.

And so, the Reverend J. A. Edmondson, having awakened all the sleeping dogs that Laramie had so carefully walked around for so long, was removed from the Laramie charge by action of the Conference Board. He was appointed to Central City, Colorado, "one of the most desirable charges in the gift of the Conference." Hayford made it a point to visit Central City when it was learned that Edmondson had married a personable young lady from Ottawa, Illinois, named Mary Donovan. He reported pleasure in the visit and his approval of the bride.

She was about "thirty years old, a gentle, refined lady who had just the right qualities to tone down the rough edges and jagged corners of the Reverend."

Hayford expressed his genuine deep regret over the loss of Edmondson. He was just as outspoken in 1879 when he wrote: "The Sentinel records without regret the departure of the Rev. J. McGaughey, late pastor of the Presbyterian Church of Laramie." No explanation of that remark has been found.

Rough and jagged as were the Edmondson corners, there was never another minister in any of Laramie's churches who so directly challenged and actively crusaded against the immorality in the Gem City which flourished with the tacit approval of its city officials.

Eleven

After the Chronicle closed down Attorney Bramel moved to Colorado's beautiful North Park. It was a short stay and his return to Laramie was even shorter. He went over the hill to Cheyenne and there entered into another newspaper venture.

Of Bramel's different newspaper efforts over the years some of Hayford-Gates' mildest remarks were in regard to Bramel and his Cheyenne Gazette:

> When we saw the paper used to pettifog his lawcases and the old patent howl about the Laramie Ring, we knew the earmarks and . . . recognized . . . the bray of the ass . . . .

Naturally with another election looming all the newspapers were red-hot with propaganda and electioneering.

In those days people took their politics as seriously as their drinking, and the mud that was thrown was very thick. The give and take was about even, but tempered with humor and much ridicule, most of it good-natured. The green poison came later when the nation assumed the mask of sophistication.

From the safety of their Cheyenne offices Bramel and Reed lit the fires and Hayford never let them go out.

He rounded on Bramel for operating his usual "smut machine" and telling the lie that "Hayford is the leader and ring master of the Republican Party." This he denied vehemently and at length in a column and a half, declaring himself as only "earnestly wanting to serve from a back seat, and working only to secure the success of the party and its principles."

On the other hand he reminded the public that Bramel had always "aspired to leadership of the Democracy." (Democracy was usually the word used to refer to the Democrat party.) Hayford also reminded the public that Bramel's cronies had "taken over the county when it was entirely out of debt and had a surplus of several thousands of dollars in the treasury, and now we find it bankrupt, the county many thousands of dollars in debt and our county warrants worth but fifty cents on the dollar."

Bill Nye, and a few other citizens, advertised their willingness to buy county warrants, hopeful that the county would soon be solvent again and would redeem the warrants at face value.

It was almost a relief during the election years to find any news item on a different subject. Of certain comic relief was the news that Brigham Young had lost his family roll-call and was terribly muddled about his children and their names. (Mormons and their beliefs in plural marriage were made much of in those days, mostly in jokes or indignation.) So, too, the entertaining fashion item of the latest in ladies petticoats made of richly-embroidered paper. Each petticoat contained an installment of the new novel by English writer Anthony Trollope entitled *"Tucks and Frills."* The story would be complete, it was stated, in 50 weekly petticoats.

One of the more titillating items concerned the notice of a widower's club in which membership was limited to gentlemen whose wives were out of town. "Now in Cheyenne" the item noted "men send their wives back east to visit their mothers" so that they then could enjoy the privileges of the club.

When Hayford was out of town J. E. Gates took over as editor. There was little difference in make-up. Gates' efforts were a bit more circumspect. It is clear that Bramel and Reed irritated Hayford and Gates to the same degree. Until Bill Nye appeared in its pages, however, the Sentinel reflected the Hayford viewpoint. As to the *Cheyenne Gazette* Hayford commented:

> Judge Andrews, Charlie Bramel and two or three other self-sacrificing patriots who are ambitious to serve the country as Delegates to Congress or (as) County officials, have succeeded in capturing the Cheyenne Hornet and Hardinge and will bring it up here (to Laramie) and then the Democrats will have a (real) organ . . . .

(At that time Doc Hayford was a Republican. Later he changed parties and he, too, became an "unterrified" Democrat, later still he returned to the Republican party.)

> . . . We only hope (the Sentinel item continued) it will be a decent, respectable sheet, a credit to our city and a promoter of intelligence, morality and harmony . . . instead of lending its influence to foster vice and promote discord . . . .

The latter was a definite swipe at Bramel over his part in the feud with the Reverend Edmondson.

Andrews apparently felt his name had been taken in vain and denied he was associated with the Bramel sheet. He sent the following epistle to the *Sentinel*:

> Editor Sentinel: My kingdom for a cane.* One suitable to chastise editors of newspapers that meddle with personal matters that do not concern the public. Would refer all such to 26th chapter of the Book of Proverbs, verses 17, 18, 19 and 20. Isaiah 50: 11.

> (signed) 'One Who Knows How It Is Himself.'

Editor's Note advised readers:

> We publish the above at Andrews' special request. We haven't time to look up the passages referred to but as he has turned his attention to reading the Bible we infer that death is staring him in the face and under these circumstances can refuse him nothing.

---

*   A reference also to the Rev. Edmondson and the cane given him for defense against Bramel.

Andrew's Bible references shed some light on the subject:

> Proverbs states: 'Like one who seizes a dog by the ears is a passer-by who meddles in a quarrel not his own. Like a madman shooting firebrands or deadly arrows is a man who deceives his neighbor and says: "I was only joking!" Without wood a fire goes out. Without gossip a quarrel dies down.'

(So easily did the gentleman forget his own feeding of the fires in the Edmondson affair.)

> Isaiah 50: 11 - 'But now all of you who light fires and provide yourselves with flaming torches go, walk in the light of your fires and of the torches you have set a- blaze. This is what you will receive from my hand: You will lie down in torment.'*

In spite of the wish for a cane to warm the Hayford back Andrews offered or consented to act as political reporter when the *Sentinel's* Editor-in-Chief was laid up in bed during the heat of the campaign.

Andrews was President of the Democrat Convention and that group had put C. W. Bramel's name up as delegate to the Legislature.

Two or three issues of the *Sentinel* carried full-column reports on the campaigns written by N. L. Andrews. His clear, balanced writings evidently surprised everyone including Hayford. He published a nice little item in the Sentinel mentioning the "fine contribution written by a Democratic Christian."

This contribution by Andrews didn't completely change the editor's criticism of the man. When Andrews became embroiled in a swindle involving some $2,000 worth of shenanigans in connection with a business establishment in Cheyenne known as the Fashion Saloon, Hayford's comments were sharp. He tempered them, however, with a mild: "We have no wish to harm

---

*   Quote from New International Version.

Andrews . . ." Perhaps he recalled the fine contribution of the "Democratic Christian" to his paper.

But it proved too much for Hayford, dipping his "teaspoon" into the editorial ink he let fly with the following:

> The Rev. Brother Edmondson ought to be here now to deliver a moral lecture about a man who occupies a high position in society, Ex-Speaker of the Legislature, Ex-Judge, leader of society, leader of his political party (who) makes some pretensions to morality, etc. But Andrews 'knows how it is' . . . .

Andrews did, indeed. He soon moved north to the Big Horn area and the town of Buffalo which stood on the border of the Fort McKinney military reservation. N. L. was to be Buffalo's first lawyer.

A short time after N. L. arrived in Buffalo a small blue-eyed blonde calling herself Nettie Wright showed up in town. She hired Andrews to collect a sum of money from one Charlie Wright, which he did. And Nettie bought property on Laurel Street and set up a business on the twilight side of propriety, and was well spoken of by many men of the town.

From all accounts Nettie was the same Nettie/Nellie Wright- Davis of Laramie's famous Crystal Wine Parlors. References to her in the *Laramie Sentinel* were both as Nettie and Nellie. On December 8, 1876, she and John Davis were married by Justice N. L. Andrews. Somehow she shed Davis before arriving in Buffalo, and the first call for help was made to the Honorable N. L. Andrews formerly of Laramie.

But back to Bramel as delegate to the Legislature and the fine contributions of political reporting to the Sentinel the editor slyly commented that "All churches are well attended. The candidates are showing their piety." A remark that fits well in later election years.

The revelation was also made to the public that the County Commissioners had accepted the uncompleted, unsigned bond of George Ritter as County Treasurer, that they had known for some time of shortages in his department, and they had knowingly approved payment more than once of the same vouchers.

Two Commissioners' seats were to be filled. There was also a battle for the Sheriff's slot. Sheriff Brophy and his one- time deputy, Lawrence Fee, were vying for that seat. Brophy had fired Fee after their tilt with Jack Watkins when both officers were injured and Watkins had got away. Now a strong letter was sent in to the paper by a supporter of Fee who reminded the public that Fee had "risked his life to save that of Brophy and had been fired for it."

There were also strong contests for the offices of Justices of the Peace.

The entire slate lost except Fee. Holliday and Durlacher stepped down as Commissioners, Ritter served eleven months of his one year sentence in the Pen, and Andrews lost his position as Justice of the Peace. Then he moved to Buffalo where he died in 1892.

Attorney I. P. Caldwell, he of the high-wheeled bicycle and flying black coat-tails, became Justice and Bill Nye won the other Justice seat. All in all the Republican Party had some rejoicing to do.

After that election Bill Nye suggested in the Sentinel that everyone should go to church and "try to offset all the wicked things you have said during the weeks about election" and admonished the electorate to "breathe through the nose from now on."

Bramel and Reed went out of the newspaper business and for a time faded into the background, and over in Colorado the Reverend J. A. Edmondson was assigned to Central City for another year.

Politics always aroused the spirits in the town, human and liquid, particularly when the question of Sunday closing cropped up, as it did with each new campaign.

One notable contest occurred in the campaigns of 1889 when Dr. Finfrock was Mayor and August Trabing sought to unseat him.

A March 2 news item reminded the public that "during the past year the affairs of the city have been well managed. Restrictions and lessening in vice and crime, gambling has been held in check, some of the 'tinhorns' and deadbeats driven from the community. Prostitutes don't splurge about the streets flaunting their vice in the face of decent women and schoolgirls as they did before. The license fees on the liquor business has been raised."

A check of the city records for 1889 shows fines were up from $10 and $13 to $20, but only keepers were being charged the higher amount, and inmates or boarders seem not to be mentioned.

The "High License Ticket" had the following slate: for Mayor – Dr. Finfrock; Alderman from First Ward – A. S. Peabody; Alderman from Second Ward – W. E. Chaplin; and Lauritz Miller was Third Ward candidate for Alderman. Otto Gramm ran for City Treasurer, C. P. Arnold for City Attorney and John (Oyster-parlor) Dimmitt for City Clerk. Chaplin and Arnold had supplied the names for the city streets when the Council decided to replace the letters with names. This was accomplished in June of that year after the spring election.

There was much chaffing and the usual frothing-at-the-mouth during this contest between Finfrock's "High-License Ticket" and Trabing's. That wily campaigner and his slate of candidates ran on what they called the Working Man's Ticket.

On March 30th the *Sentinel* carried the following advice:

A. Trabing is an energetic, wide awake man, a wholesale and retail liquor dealer. And it is a most important branch of his business. The saloon men (in town) are among his largest customers.

And on another page:

... a prominent candidate on the so-called labor ticket said to the editor: 'I expect the support of the liquor dealers, gamblers, pimps, prostitutes and workingmen.'

This slate ran on the following platform:

We are for high and restrictive license for all of the business houses paying government license for the sale of liquor, including drug stores, and wholesale and retail liquor dealers. Saloons to keep orderly houses or forfeit their license. Absolute abolition of gambling in the city of Laramie. Reduction of taxation by careful management of city affairs. Employment of old and tried residents for all city work.

The disbelieving editor of the *Sentinel* remarked:

"Now this platform reads well enough and as the men who (may be) elected on it are honorable and reliable, we feel justified in assuming that they will carry out in good faith the principles upon which they ask for votes. If they do this there will be no just complaint.

Trabing's ticket won by two to one. The "Working Man's Ticket" were prepared for victory and a grand parade of banners and draped buggies led by a brass band and happy, shouting pedestrians did the town until the wee hours of the morning. The usual boys, afoot and on bicycles, adorned the edges of the moving crowd and the usual excited dogs added their voices to the din. The Working Man's Ticket kept its word but lost out at the next election and the *Weekly Sentinel* lamented:

The resignation of Mr. Kingsford and election of John Mast gives the Democrats absolute control of the city government. Ordinances have (now) been passed allowing saloons to stay open on Sunday and to license gambling.

This action rescinded the ordinance passed in 1889 by A. Trabing to eliminate gambling and putting high license on liquor sales and on prostitution. Thus the pendulum swung and the city was back again with its "necessary evils."

The argument put forth by liquor dealers was that if saloons were again open on Sunday the amount of consumption there was less than it would be at home, or on the street. Their premise was that the company of other men with their drinks slowed down the quaffing because of the visiting over their cups, and the bartender "could limit the drinks. Whereas if liquor is sold to go the drinker can drink as he wills."

The argument from the other side reminded the public of the number of "riots, street robberies and home burglaries allowed to go on in the interest of a lot of dead beats, whiskey bummers and grogsellers."

There had been a confusion of such occurrences that spring and the newsmen were agreed that "... if the law and authorities refuse to grant protection we advise the victims to fall back on shotguns."

In March, 1881, the first issue of the *Daily Boomerang* had been published with Edgar Wilson (Bill) Nye as managing editor.

In a letter written in 1924 by Henry Wagner to W. E. Chaplin, Laramie newspaperman, but living and working then in Cheyenne, Wagner relates how he helped raise funds to start the *Boomerang*:

> I asked Nye if he would be willing to operate a daily newspaper. He said yes. I told him to come back about two o'clock and I'd let him know. I went to see A. S. Peabody, the Trabing Brothers, Robert Marsh, Will Holliday and others, and among us we raised $3,000 to finance the enterprise.

> When the press came I gave the upstairs over my clothing store adjoining the Wyoming National Bank (for operating rooms.) It proved a grand success. But Bill Nye's health failed and he left for Greeley Colorado.

The *Daily Boomerang*, named for Nye's intelligent mule, proved to be a worthy competitor to the Sentinel. Too, it seemed to move around quite a bit, and seemed to have an affinity for stables.

It occupied, for a time, quarters in a rickety old house – probably after Wagner moved to Denver, then later moved to the upper floor of Anderson's livery barn at the corner of Third and Garfield, east of the old Frontier Hotel.

The *Weekly Sentinel* of August 30, 1890, announced a new location for the paper:

> Bill Nye's old mule Boomerang is going to be moved into Mr. Ivinson's stable tomorrow where he will stand during the balance of the season . . . .

The paper was printed in the old haymow there for a number of years. Ivinson's stable was on the west side of the alley on South A (Ivinson) next to Kuster's Hotel. At this date the Ivinsons had moved from their second street flat over the bank out to the corner of Sixth and Grand. In a handsome building which had been moved in from Fort Sanders and set up on the corner east of the courthouse, the Ivinsons lived until their own palatial house was completed in the summer of 1892. Thus the Ivinsons escaped the fevers and flavors of the front streets and embarked on a grander scale of living.

It was always claimed that the effluvium of the barns rising to the press rooms caused the illness of Nye and other employees of the paper. So Nye was forced to leave Laramie for a wider world and fame.

Twelve

The claim has been made that the railroad men had spawned the western low-life and vice dens and bordellos for the edification of those who followed. But when the railroaders and fabled Gandy dancers were gone and the lumbermen had stripped the forested hills, there remained the miners, cowboys, shop workers and townsmen — and traveling salesmen. It is doubtful if any of these needed instruction in what news sheets referred to as "this necessary evil."

Advertisements appeared in newspapers of the day addressed to the male of the species. They offered a cure to "men suffering from the errors and indiscretions of youth, nervous weakness, early decay and loss of manhood." The cure supposedly had been discovered by a missionary to South America and was offered by two different clergymen on the east coast.

From certain sly newspaper items concerning men between divorces or deaths of wives and re-marriage, it appears that many of them never missed a trick on the Front Streets. It supposedly was proof (or assurance) of manhood.

These sporting men had numerous derogatory names for the women they used. Terms for men caught up in their phallic worship are less well known.

There was a frequent haranguing against the bawdy houses and their inmates, accompanied by such remarks as "we trust the evil will not trouble our authorities again soon."

If it ever had.

One of the grievances in Laramie was the easy treatment extended to keepers of brothels: a stern lecture and fine for the madams and usually a change of venue for the panders, which assured them a sympathetic judge and sometimes opportunity for a bit of quiet bribery.

In medieval times it was thought that only men suffered from what was called "love-sickness." The cure then was simple — and universal: get married or sleep frequently with beautiful women, changing partners as often as possible. Many did both.

When it was discovered that women also "learned to suffer" from the erogenous disease it was branded hysteria. The cure for women was to find distraction in games, food, music and frequent baths.

Anne Ellis wrote in her book "The Life Of An Ordinary Woman": "Women dream many dreams and see many visions while bending over a washtub."

The dreams and visions may have represented the wishful side, but the washtub certainly presented the practical and probably provided quicker and more lasting cures.

In a contemporary issue, the Sentinel published an item labeled "A New Departure." It affirms that women had considered rebellion from time to time away back . . .

A soldier had presented the clipping (from an unnamed source) to the Sentinel and it was just the sort of improbable thing to delight the western gentlemen:

> A lady correspondent discourses: 'The great want of women at present is money — money for their personal wants and money to carry out their plans. I propose that they shall earn it, that they shall consider it as honorable to work for as for board, and demand equal pay for (equal) work.
>
> 'I insist that the bearing and rearing of children (the most exacting of employments and involving the most terrible risks) shall be the best paid work in the world, and that husbands shall treat their wives with at least as much consideration and money as wet nurses.

'The meaning of all this is, that wives are about to strike for greenbacks, so much for every baby born. No greenbacks, no more sons and daughters; no more population, no more boys to carry on the great enterprise of the age.

'The scale of prices for maternal duties are as follows: girl baby, $100; boy, $200; twins, $300; both boys, $400; triplets, $600; triplets, all boys $1,000. MOTTO: Pay up or dry up. Terms, C.O.D. No credit beyond first child. Husbands who desire to transmit their names to posterity will please take notice, and take a new departure.'

Ordinarily men, and western men in particular, are patted on the back for their courteous and respectful treatment of women in general, "good" women in particular.

The scarcity of women in the west determined their relationships with men. No matter the "equality" of women in Wyoming there was often a difference between their public treatment and what they received at home. Publicly they received deference and respect, but that didn't keep them from being slapped around at home when the mister's disposition was showing.

One of the few rough-handers ever sent to jail in Laramie for that pastime was Ben F. Smith, "the well-known wife beater." He was fined $100 and sentenced to six months in jail. He threatened suicide. Hayford suggested the county furnish the rope.

His wife bought the Tivoli-Centennial saloon and soon took to the bottle. She was later arrested for drunkenness, put into jail and discovered dead in her cell the following morning. Booze had long been used as a painkiller. There was no inquest and little comment in the paper.

She had earlier (1892) sold the saloon to John Huempfner, Laramie's "Beer King." He tore down the historic frame building and put up the present brick edifice at 111 Grand.

Actually the Smith incident was not an isolated one, nor can it be accepted as a general occurrence. Court cases do cite a number of wife and child beatings and mistreatment in that era. The frequent use of scorn or ridicule was as demeaning as the fist, and less noticeable, something that has not changed with time. It is referred to as "incompatibility" in divorce courts ....

Hayford's newspaper comments in announcing new births show that his male pride was more pronounced when the baby was a boy. On occasion his comments on an "increase in the family" were tasteless and fatuous. In that period a pregnant woman was seldom seen in public, and being in a "delicate" or "interesting condition" was treated with special gallantry for it was evident that she had pleased her husband.

The bearing of children, of course, plays havoc with the "womanly shape" and harsh weather is no kinder to her complexion. A beauty column of the day recommended that women should follow the practice of Diane dePoitiers, mistress of Henry II, who at age 67 "looked no older than 25." The writer remarked that the lady did not use cosmetics, had daily baths in cold water and rode horseback for an hour every day. "If women of the present day would woo nature and reject cosmetics they would not look old and haggard at age 40."

If Diane had been introduced to mop and washtub and a daily routine of diapers, croup and family care along with regular housework, she would have looked all of 67 at age 40.

There was quite a difference between the whore and the married woman. The whore was available for a man's passing fancy and not expected to wash and mend his clothes nor cook his meals, bear his children or nurse and mother him in his ills or in his cups. Nor did she bear his name and meet with the respect usually engendered on the street and among society. The whore lived on by-streets and lent an ear to man-troubles and shared certain moments stolen from his wife and family. And that was accepted by the public — as a "necessary evil."

Not all those times and/or hours away from home were spent in the back streets and alley cribs, however. In the centuries-old, unchanging times before social clubs replaced the public tavern and grogshop they who went there went to drink in company of other men, with results often staggering. If the customer had troubles, or thought he had, there was the bar to lean on and willing ears to talk into. And the thirsty one was there to imbibe and "forget." If he had lost his job he'd often take the last pay check and drown his feelings of inadequacy or anger among other men. Or, if he felt like a turn at cards or dice, he'd gamble on that. No matter that wife and family were home facing the same problems, he had to forget.

All the hard drinking was not confined to saloons and/or parlor houses, nor was it confined only to men. Women were just as beset with problems and decisions and the same wish to forget. Many of those in bawdy houses, aware that their lives held no promises, and any number in their homes, aware of the same hopeless future, alike but different. Any number of women died, victim as much of the loneliness of marriage as of the "unwise use of alcohol."

While the mister hung elbows over bar or table, his wife sat home trying to figure ways to stretch the food in the house, or trying, by kerosene lamp, to find the relaxation her man found so attractive elsewhere. If she drank herself to death, gossip and newspapers said so in condemning words. When a man died of the same symptoms the words were more often sympathetic. He had "business reverses" or "family troubles" and took to liquor. It was "an unfortunate waste of a good man" (or life). On some occasions the world was "better off without such as he."

Not all drinking was of hard liquors. Fresh and dried fruits were to be had from any store in town. Dried fruit kept well, and much of it found its way into a sweet cordial or frumenti well favored by householders. The same mixture of fermented fruits a century later is made into a delicious cake and graces the tables of homes that do not countenance liquors of any kind.

It was thought that the crib or parlor girls, being of such depraved natures, naturally took to drink. Some took opium or morphine or other drugs, mostly as painkiller, and not for the out-of-body experiences that later became the fad. It apparently was accepted that these "girls" took such medications. So when Dora Marr and Sallie Thixton committed suicide with morphine it was of little moment. "Crazy Jane" Hart resorted to laudanum. Fanny Rolly shot herself after her small daughter died.

Clara Gilmore, one of Minnie Ford's flock, only had a bad case of tonsillitis, so no doctor went to see her at 311 Front Street. She took morphine to ease the pain. The drug caused the tissues of her throat to swell and she suffocated. The obituary notice said death was caused by the use of morphine. The coroner's inquest detailed her intense suffering from what probably was strep throat or quinsy.

When a handsome young woman died in a house of ill fame on Second Street the Sentinel stated "Miss Ida White died of that terrible disease consumption." Miss Ida complained about that and the next day a correction appeared: The dead woman was Ella Williams whose husband had deserted her a year ago, left her penniless and without friends. No one would help her. "All that was left for her was a life of shame."

There are many true tales of "fallen women" with hearts of gold. There are other tales of women too tender of heart to make a choice for fear someone's feelings would be hurt. Then there are those with other interests. An unusual incident occurred one summery April day on South A. Street.

Two "way-up gemm'en", calling on a courtesan, met at her front door. They began to argue over who was to go in. Number One chased Number Two across the street, around a signboard in front of Gramm's Drugstore, knocking down a third man on one of the rounds. Man No. 3 caught No. 2 and began "pounding him frightfully." No. 2 pulled a gun and began to fire haphazardly. No. 1 shot at No. 2 until he staggered and fell, then he fired two or three more rounds to be on the safe side.

A soldier, passing by, saved caller No. 2 who was badly beaten and had two bullet holes in him. Dr. Harris was called and said he thought the man might live. On-lookers were more interested in the pattern of bullet holes in the sign and spared scarcely a twinge or squeam for the beaten man.

The lady whose favors were sought testified she had not witnessed the occurrence since she was busy in her parlor with some needlework.

Man No. 1 was sent to prison, served his time and went to Colorado where he later was hanged for lot-jumping.

Another less humorous incident roused the entire town, partly because it involved two lawmen from Greeley. Such things, as Brother Andrews had insisted, gave the town a bad name. And the serious part which brought the kettle to a full boil was the involvement of Nellie/Nettie Wright and Pawnee Liz.

Marriage to John Davis had not affected Nellie Wright's career at the Crystal Wine Parlors. The accusation that she operated a bagnio brought her outraged response that she did not "keep no bagnio, nor any other kind of house, only an old invalid who pays her for her care of him."

The entire affair has a peculiar smell and the reporting of it is confusing.

The Crystal Wine Parlor was located on Front Street probably in the old Mayflower Saloon near the Borgemeier-Theis blacksmith shop. On the other side of the alley were the back doors of Caira Simpson's dressmaker shop, of Fagan's Alhambra Saloon and the brothers' first store.

The incident supposedly occurred in Nellie's place.

Two lawmen from Greeley, named Richard Davis and William S. Mullion, were in Laramie looking for a criminal wanted in Colorado and had stopped off at Nellie's. Mullion became involved in an argument with an associate of one William T. Schell or Schnell. The argument grew heated and Mullion removed his coat to fight the other man who was not named.

Schnell at once took Mullion's coat to hold and began rifling the pockets. Davis ordered him to stop. Schnell removed Mullions pocketbook and ran. The two Colorado men dashed after him, both shooting and calling out "Stop!"

Schnell was hit but ran on down the alley back of Fagan's saloon. He fell but got up running and disappeared into the darkness. He later was found in the railroad yards, dead, with four bullets in him.

The event occurred in the joint on Front Street, yet the Colorado men were immediately "arrested in the house of Elizabeth Stevens" which was on C Street three blocks away.

There was a hearing before Judge Donnellan. N. R. Davis "one of the largest stockmen of northern Colorado, came from his Owl Creek ranch to assist his brother and Mullion. And J. W. Fetterman, Esq., a Greeley attorney, arrived to defend the two Greeley men."

Their presence was unnecessary as it turned out, for Donnellan had already acquitted the two.

With the Greeley attorney singing the praises of the Laramie judge for his legal expertise and fairness, the four Colorado men left town. As to Schnell, who had once worked as foreman of Stanley brothers ranch on Rock Creek, it was learned that he was a notorious outlaw, and "public opinion held that the community was well rid of one of its most dangerous criminals." Then the Sentinel said further:

How much Pawnee Liz has cost the county . . . in ruined youth . . . demoralized and rendered unfit to be husbands and fathers and decent members of society . . .

How much money has gone into her dive which should have gone to the grocer, to the dry goods and clothing merchant, and to pay honest debts and clothe dependents. The Sheriff's courts, police magistrates, etc. could count up to her credit a large amount of money.

Albany County annually pays $50,000 in taxes and several thousand in licenses and at least 90% of it goes to support or punish paupers and criminals, nearly everyone of whom is chargeable to these necessary evils.

There was no further mention of Nellie Wright and her bagnio, possibly because her husband Davis was a respected business man. Possibly, too, because it wasn't long after this that Nellie left town and moved herself and her activities north to Buffalo. There she became involved with two soldiers from Fort McKinney in the theft of arms and ammunition from the U.S. government. Nellie, known as Nettie Stewart in Buffalo, was brought to Laramie for trial.

The petite blonde invoked the names of N. L. Andrews and several well-known men-about-Laramie as character references. The pretty little lady was promptly acquitted. Her companions in crime were not.

Thirteen

The town was never far removed from its shadowy half-world.

The newspapers of March, 1883 reported the arrest and trial of Camille Gayotte who had put in a dance hall at Cummins City and "came into town looking for recruits."

Cummins City was a gold-mining town about thirty miles southwest of Laramie near the Colorado border. It was locally famous for the swindle of shareholders in gold mines that had been salted. Otherwise it was a typical mountain town high up toward the source of the Big Laramie River.

Gayotte, in his recruiting trip to Laramie, had enticed a twelve-year-old girl to go with him by "making promises, giving her a nice ring, a new hat and new shoes, and getting her drunk." Her name was Bridget.

Her father was a laborer at the soda works making no more than three dollars a day, if that much. With several other members in the family it is plain they didn't live extravagantly.

Bridget's father swore out a warrant and had the flesh-broker arrested. The trial judge, Groesbeck, fined the pander $100 — "the limit of the law" the judge said, and released him. Later Gayotte was indicted along with W. H. Johnson. Johnson did not appear in court in spite of the order to his sureties to "bring the body of the said W. H. Johnson into court as provided in their bond."

Gayotte was tried and the verdict returned read "Guilty as in the indictment charged." There was no mention of his crime against a child, and the jury recommended him to the clemency of the court. He was sentenced to be "confined in the common jail of Albany County for the term of four months."

Bridget's sentence was for life, branded and ostracized.

The *Sentinel* professed outrage and declared:

> Papa should have settled the worthless whelp with a shotgun. The law should have sentenced him to life in the penitentiary, and failing that the community ought to have hung him.

Nothing of the sort happened, of course.

The community, while professing righteous indignation, horror and outrage, found no time for the child. She returned home to face the shame and anger of her family, the avid curiosity of the community, and probably jeers and harassment from former friends and classmates as well as sly advances from men, young and old.

Much less fuss was made over the demoralization of a twelve- year-old girl than there had been after the two mature men were apprehended in the house of ill repute owned by Nellie/Nettie Wright.

Apparently the stigma of Cummins City was greater than that of Front Street for the good-folk of town. Wherever Bridget turned there was no help. Life at home was not the same. She left and went to Cheyenne where, according to Hayford, they bragged they had thirty-nine prostitutes.

For nearly two years Bridget remained in Cheyenne and "made herself a holy terror to the police there." She spent much of that time in jail. What better way to have warmth, food and lodging? At last the Cheyenne authorities shipped her back to Laramie, and Hayford "recommended her to the special care of (city) Marshall Erisman." Nowhere was a place for her except in the community she wanted to escape.

Bridget is mentioned in the newspapers once more when she "swallowed an ounce of laudanum and died at the coon dive of Felix Monroe on the west side where she had been living for some time past."

There was no inquest. No obituary. No record of burial in the cemetery.

Bridget was barely eighteen.

But all the panting was not done on Front Street. On Third Street were Sophia Riccard, Kate Frost and Josephine Demer, and scattered about other side streets and out on East Grand, and even in the most staid neighborhoods were accommodations.

Away from the razzle-dazzle of Front Street and its environs stood what was referred to as a "rookery in a core part of the city's residential district." The location was on South B (Grand) and Third Street where brick "blocks" now line the street.

In December, 1880, James W. Ingersoll made two sales of portions of lots on that corner. The east (Third Street side) thirty-eight feet of the north three lots of the block were sold to blacksmith Nicholas Theis, former partner of Borgemeier over on Front Street. Theis set up his shop on the new site and hung up his sign, a giant horse-shoe.

The west 94 feet of the three lots went to a Mrs. Dollie Baillie. She didn't need to put out a sign, for she was a "woman of known reputation."

She had several names besides Dollie; Chrissy Branch, Puss Newport, The Blonde, Christy Grover and Mrs. John A. Grover. It was said that she had previously been a "boarder" in Cheyenne's famous "House of Mirrors."

Here, on Grand Avenue, between the Theis blacksmith shop and the alley, the Blond had two houses built. The first was a four room affair added to the rear of a four-room house once used (back in 1868-'69) for Sunday School classes. The other consisted of six rooms, a kitchen, parlor, four bedrooms and a wide hallway. Inventory of the furnishings in this house show satin covered chairs, a tête-tête in rose satin, carpets, a new Fischer upright piano, marble-top walnut stands and other fine walnut pieces in the parlor which was warmed by a coal-burning heating stove and lighted by coal- oil lamps with "fancy shades." Each of the bedrooms was furnished with "fine walnut suits (sic) and other falal."

A review of a number of her grocery slips (charged at the Trabing Brothers' Blue Front Store on First Street, and at Peabody's on Second) shows that some of The Blonde's intimate dinners were gourmet affairs with rarities such as eels, lamb, artichokes, oysters, celery, fine cheeses and beer. Always cheese and beer.

The *City Directory of 1875* shows that John Grover was working as a salesman in that year and boarding at Henry Wagner's on Fourth and A Street.

A July 2, 1877 *Sentinel* news item reports that John A. Grover, and wife and child had returned from a visit in Maine.

"Wife and child" are nowhere mentioned again. There is no record in Laramie of that marriage, no record of divorce, and no record of death or burial in the town's cemetery records.

On July 7, 1877, Grover bought the Ora Haley meat market. He fitted it out in fine style, installing a cold room for meats. Hayford went to look it over. Grover demonstrated how it worked by shutting the editor in. Within a few minutes Hayford was glad to be allowed to step out, admitting it was a fine meat-keeper.

In 1879, John A. Grover, a single man whose absence would be "mourned by a number of young ladies," left Laramie for Leadville, Colorado and its fortune-laden fields. In November, 1880, Grover and partner Simon Jones dissolved their partnership in the store. Grover sold his share to a man named Mansfield and thereafter it was known as the "People's Market, Jones and Mansfield, Props."

In September, 1881, John A. Grover and Christy A. Finlayson, both of Laramie, were married in Denver and returned to Laramie and to her home on Grand Avenue. It was better known as "The Blonde's", and Christy better known as Dollie Baillie, or Puss Newport, and other aliases. Christy ran the show at her place with at least three young women under her management. Grover set up a saloon on the northwest corner of South A and Second Street, across from the old site of the Big Tent.

In December, "Miss Arlington", one of the frail sisters in The Blonde's menage, was tried for larceny of $75 from one Daniel Lynch. The same day Grover and his partner Grove Pittman were put under $400 bonds charged with keeping a gambling house.

On February 15, 1882, Christy Grover, age 30, shot herself in the head with her husband's revolver, which was always kept loaded in their bedroom.

Christy's suicide was reported in scathing words:

Last Sunday evening about 6 o'clock, Mrs. John A. Grover, alias Mrs. D. Bailey, alias Puss Newport, alias "The Blonde", a noted Cyprian of this city, committed suicide by shooting herself in the head . . . . There is little use to which such wrecks on the shores of time can be put, except to serve as beacon lights to warn other Voyagers . . . . We have no knowledge of the past life and history of this woman, but it is not probable she had . . . Christian parents and was brought up under good and wise training. It is not our prerogative to judge her.

Then the Editor goes ahead with his judgement:

She has lived a life of vice and crime, leaving the trail of the serpent wherever she went sowing the seeds of death and dragging others down with her, and such a death is a fitting death to such a life.

At the coroner's inquest Grover testified that he and Mrs. Grover had "gone driving that afternoon, had gone to the Brewery, had two or three beers, had played a few games of pool, had another beer or two and returned home in the late afternoon. Mrs. Grover had gone into their house and he had put up the team and buggy."

When he came into the house Mrs. Grover was in heated discussion with Miss Arlington. Their argument centered about "the girl who had left here recently." When Grover entered the room Monte Arlington left, saying she would discuss it tomorrow, and Mrs. Grover accused her of conspiring to steal from her.

Christy then had told Grover to "go over to the other house and get warm," and she went to their bedroom. Grover heard the shot and dashed back to their house where he found Christy.

The girl referred to was one Ada Jeanette (Nettie) B. Williams who had gone to Denver in December and failed to return. She wore a fine sealskin sacque and hat. In January Mrs. Grover, using her name of Miss Newport, sent Sheriff N. K. Boswell after Nettie and the capelet and hat. Value of the furs was set at $218. The newspaper reported the incident, adding "both are women of easy virtue." Witnesses in the case were Dollie Baillie (Mrs. Grover), Monte Arlington and N. K. Boswell.

After Mrs. Grover's suicide, Mamie Hall, another of the girls managed by Christy, brought suit against the Madam's estate for "two diamonds set into gold rings" valued at $275, and one sealskin coat valued at $250, which Miss Hall claimed Mrs. Grover had given to her. Miss Hall claimed the gifts had been withheld from her by Mr. Grover. The suit was dismissed "because Miss Hall does not state sufficient facts."

In the absence of a will, the appraisers of the estate recommended that all real property, chattels and jewelry be turned over at once to John A. Grover as husband and sole heir of the deceased, lest "it be lost or otherwise dispersed."

So Grover came into property worth well over $4,000.

He continued to live in the Grand Avenue house. Assignations continued with regular callers stopping by. There is no record of how many occupants lived there. Miss Arlington and Grover apparently got along rather well. In October, 1883 they were married in Laramie. She gave her name as Mamie Lambert and age as 24. Grover was 32.

Laramie's first uniformed police force (1889). Mayor August Trabing center front, policeman Hance to his right (white beard) John Eslinger on Trabing's left. Behind the Mayor is City Marshal Clark, to his left is James Stirling, to Clark's right is Nicolas Theis. Eslinger resigned Feb. 6, 1890 - moved to Salt Lake City and joined police force out there. Theis quit April 29, 1890 and went to work in the rolling mills.

Courtesy of U. W. Research & Frye.

Looking west, along University Avenue, from the tower of "Old Main," 1901. The Ivinson mansion is in center left, penitentiary building is at center top.

Courtesy of American Heritage Center, S. H. Knight Collection, University of Wyoming.

Laramie, about 1882 - '83. The markings on this photograph are in error. Looking up Third Street (toward northeast) from the roof of the Anderson Stable at Third and Garfield (Key Bank Site). Cabins in foreground are site of Pawnee Liz's cribs. East side of Third, H. D. Beemer Paint Shop with Maennorchor Hall next door on left. Root's Opera House middle of next block, next door (to left) is Elkhorn Livery Barn, Epicopal Church roof showing beyond. On Grand Avenue (east-west street) is the Roman Catholic Church. Tall Italianate house with cupola on roof (right) is August Trabing dwelling, Trabing barn roof is visible behind Maennorchor Hall.

Courtesy of Western History Research Center, University of Wyoming.

Callaghan's Blacksmith and Wagon Shop.
Later part of Minnie Ford's bordello.

Courtesy of Western History Research Center,
University of Wyoming.

Hiskey house in front. M. C. Brown house, shed and barn connected, center of photo. A. G. Dunn house, (present Rectory) beyond Brown's.. Note drainage ditch along side of street and out houses in yards. "Old Main" at top center of picture.

Beery Collection

Laramie
Brewery.

Courtesy of
Laramie Plains
Museum.

Elmer Lovejoy's ballon-tired gasoline buggy brought Henry ford to Laramie. East Side school in background. 1905.

Courtesy of Mike Stoesz, ©Mike stoesz, Clint Rogers.

Fourteen

In the *Laramie Daily Sentinel* of May 28, 1887 the following quote appeared, taken from the *Greeley Colorado Tribune*:

> The beautiful lady of the mountains has a dirty spot on her face, not an accidental smirch but a gnawing old nastiness that has been growing fouler and fouler year by year for long years back.
>
> On a core corner of town stands a crazy tumbledown rookery full from cellar to shingles of liquor, gambling devices and everything that may be used to corrupt and rob men. Ruffians and tinhorn gamblers make night and day hideous with their orgies.
>
> A half block away on the principal residential street under the same management is a houseful of shameless women as vile, if possible, as the men who support them.
>
> Whilst Grover's Institute and its ilk are running Laramie the beautiful University of Wyoming will never be filled with students. It does determine whether she shall be the city of the plains like Sodom of old with too few decent people to be worthy of saving or whether she shall be truly 'The Gem City of the Rockies.'

(signed) J. J. Stevens.

Stevens was a former resident of Laramie, a dealer in feeds and grains. His residence had been at 612 Grand.

The *Sentinel* replied in shame:

> It's all true ... We've asked them (the Council) to refuse to license these places, and enforce the laws against selling liquors to minors and to keep them out of the gambling hells of this city. We've asked them to drive pimps and prostitutes out of the heart of the city and keep them off the public thoroughfares or make the city too hot to hold them.

We've asked them to compel these disgraceful places to close up on Sunday and at a decent hour in the evening, and don't license any more gambling hells or games than they are compelled to do by the laws of the Territory.*

In 1886 Harry Hynds of Cheyenne had opened a gambling saloon in Laramie and other towns along the U. P.. His activities and control kept the question of gambling before the public and on the election ballots. In the process all worms in the can were exposed. When the "open" administration was in power all things were allowed. When the "closed" ordinance was in effect the vices went under cover.

Any number of gaming rooms and other activities were continued in alley buildings and hidden places. One rural joint that operated well after 1900 was located out of town where Highway 30 branches off to Sybille Canyon and the Laramie Mountains via Morton Pass. The place was known as Triangle Tavern.

In one gesture made by city Authorities a "notorious resort was pulled in by city police and a lot of gamblers, prostitutes and pimps gathered in. The whole fraternity rallied and swore each other clear," the *Sentinel* reported. "They then circulated a petition demanding the removal of policeman McIntosh for not 'standing in' with them."

Across the street from Grover's Rookery, on the east side of Third, was the skating rink, in the building once the centre for the Maennorchor Society. Down the block south of the "Institute" were private residences where Jeanette Demer, Kate Frost and others welcomed callers. Sophia Piccard and Belle Warden were indicted for keeping houses of ill-shape. The language of the courts was still a bit sensitive in naming certain activities and their arenas of action.

---

*   Wyoming Territory was not admitted to the Union as a state until July, 1890.

Across the alley from the houses of evening was a boarding house and laundry, and in the alley south of the boarding house was a private residence. The "core residential area" was well populated.

These activities at Grover's occurred during one of the pendulum swings toward Sunday closings. Since gambling and drinking were legal in the Territory, and individual towns made their own rules on the subject, apparently nothing was done to shut down such places permanently and the Institute continued to operate at full swing.

In June, 1895, Miss Arlington (the third Mrs. Grover) was under indictment by the U. S. Postal Inspector. The reason was not given, but understandably she was worried and upset. District Court Journals reveal that Monte had been in the habit of sending for choice liquors from her husband's saloon then selling the booze to customers. She was indicted for selling liquor without a license. "If she had given the booze to the customer she'd never have been bothered."

This double trouble with the law, and other gnawing problems at home, it was said, caused her to suddenly "develop an aversion for food, (she) would eat only a few bites and declare herself full or not hungry." In August she refused to touch food at all and would only drink a sip or two of water. The doctors were baffled. In October she died "of insanity due to starvation." One wonders did she fear being poisoned? Or since her husband was declared not guilty of the same license offense at the same hearings and did not help her in her difficulties cause her sudden fears? Grover had been exonerated of blame in Christy's death. Wives could not be required to testify against their husbands, but did Grover think she might — ?

The short report of her demise refers to her as Mamy Grover. She is buried in Greenhill Cemetery as Mrs.

Monte Grover. There is no stone. She lies the second space beyond Christy Grover. She was 37.

So once again John A. Grover was a single man of substance.

He bought Lot No. 17 in the 300 block on Front Street where once the Borgemeier-Theis Blacksmith and Wagon Shop did business. The building was a two-story brick. Next to it were the two or three frame buildings, important in the history of Laramie City. One was Nellie Wright's Crystal Wine Parlors. The other was the National Theatre where the first women- jurors heard cases, and was now the warehouse of the Trabing Commercial Company.

Grover's brick house carried the address of 311 First Street. Grover gave this as his place of residence even though he leased the building to Minnie Ford for a period of two years at $65 per month, and renewed the lease every two years thereafter.

Minnie was a Madam, and a fixture on Front Street and her activities seem to have escaped the close scrutiny by press and city authorities that had been given to her predecessors, at least until a "dusky maiden" (as one newspaper called her), named Suzy Parker appeared on the scene.

The personable Suzy and her husband lived at First and Kearney. Even before Mr. Parker died, it didn't take long for neighbors to notice comings and goings at odd hours day or night over at the Parker corner.

First there were rumors, then reports, then there were complaints. Then there were appearances in court by the dark lady. The same pattern of dealing with her activities was followed that had been usual in earlier years with other court appearances. The current authorities apparently saw nothing irregular going on around First Street. They visited the places, collected fines and turned them in to the city. They listened to complaints, advised complaintants to put their concerns in writing and send them to the city offices. This practice was followed well into the twentieth century.

In 1903 City Marshall "informed the court that the City Council had instructed him not to enforce an ordinance or make complaint against any person or agent for renting a house for use as house of prostitution, and that City Attorney, C. P. Arnold, did not think that the laws should be enforced where they relate to prostitutes."

The City Council granted Suzy the right to hang up a red lantern. Since this privilege was not given to other brothels (legally) in town, the act was criticized by all who learned of it, especially by her immediate neighbors. But business at the corner house improved to the point that the whole neighborhood objected to the noise. One irate neighbor woman shot out the red light and the vigilant authorities hauled Suzy into court. The decision, in the face of the uproar, was that the lady must close up shop.

For weeks Suzy and four of her companions in vice waited in the town jail while her attorney, M. C. Brown, filed their writ of objection. It wasn't fair, she stated, that she should have to close when only a few blocks away other houses were allowed to operate.

The authorities hedged. The two matters were different, they stated. The other places were not in residential areas, but if they allowed Suzy to continue would she build a board fence around her place? Of course she would, and did. This shut out the sight of lascivious and flagrant sinning, but not the sounds. The objections rose to an uproar again.

Then when a young girl was accosted and dragged to a hidden corner, the attack set off a new wave of outrage.

"Suzy must go!" was the decision in press and on street.

The personable Suzy filed objection and sat in jail awaiting the trial. But public opinion was too strong so the case was moved out of town to the mountain village called Holmes in the Snowy Range. Victor Carlin was Justice of the Peace out there. He went as easy as the law allowed, but ruled that Suzy must close, and she said she would.

Suzy's fence effectively cut off sight of any and all activities at her place, but there were visitors seen dropping in, for watchers were many. Some, to the horror of the public, were "seen going into the place even in broad daylight and staying for an hour or two."

So the rumors flew that she was still operating. Suzy denied it before the judge. She was a "good girl', she said, doing as she had been told.

Suddenly the town sprang to alert and indignant attention. The rumor now noised about was that Suzy had bought or leased property in the 300 block of First Street, next to Minnie Ford's house. The indignation became anger: That was the white area and Suzy had no right — !

The rumors persisted for a time then abruptly died. Suzy was scarcely heard of again, although when she applied for license to operate some years later, it was denied.

Suzy, as did other property owners in her block, sold her holdings to the Union Pacific Railroad Company. The buildings were cleared away, and the new passenger depot was later build where Suzy's house of ill-fame had stood.

John A. Grover remained in the "white" district, living at 311 First Street where Minnie Ford operated. Grover ran his saloon on South A, and the "rookery with its cellar to eaves full of gambling devices" also continued to operate.

Nothing appears to have resulted from the condemnation of J. J. Stevens.

Of course gambling was legal in the Territory, and by law licenses must be granted to applicants. The question that often arose, though, was how many? Nor did there seem to be restriction on the number of liquor licenses granted. The city did, however, manage to remove all drinking places to one general area.

Shortly after the turn of the century John A. Grover went to California. He made two or three return visits to Laramie then went to stay. The reason given was ill health. As mysterious as his marriages and the ends of them, so is his business or other activities in California.

Public records of Albany County show that in 1909 Grover sold the Grand Avenue property to Edwin A. Wilkinson, Laramie insurance agent. Within a matter of weeks Wilkinson had re-sold the property with its improvements to W. E. Chaplin, Frank Spafford and James Mathison and they set up the *Republican* newspaper plant there. From this address, they had impishly reported the "pro" side of Suzy and her antics. The *Daily Boomerang* roundly berated the "Grand Avenue Rag" for its attitudes and comments regarding the whole affair, overlooking the permissiveness of city officials on that subject for a quarter century. The *Republican* later published from quarters across the street.

On April 16, 1912, in Los Angeles, California, John A. Grover, bed-ridden and partially paralyzed, rigged up a shotgun to his bed-frame and killed himself.

There were no known immediate relatives other than a half- brother in Maine. The Court ruled that Grover's entire Laramie holdings should go to him. Then wife number four entered her claim from Los Angeles. She produced proof of marriage and a will dated in August, 1904. After some deliberation the wife and the half-brother reached amicable agreement and shared equally in the estate. All property was sold, including that on First Street. Minnie Ford's lease was terminated. Seven years later Suzy Parker got her heart's desire, to own property in the "accepted" red-light district. She operated a regular boarding house.

So John Grover died, a victim of "youthful excesses and decay." Perhaps he never read advertisements, especially those of South American missionaries.

Fifteen

Coal-oil lighting made little impression on the night's darkness. Night walkers moved from shadows to deeper shadows and although the early-day thugs and high-rollers were gone there were still enough of the element remaining to make the streets of Laramie unsafe at night. Thus the introduction of artificial gas in 1884 was greeted with delight. It was adopted by many business houses. Trabing's mammoth store at Second and South C "glowed from basement to turret" with hissing gas jets. And for the first time there were street lights. tall cast-iron poles topped with large glass globes.

Not everyone put in gas, however, for there was talk of electricity and electric power, a promise of better lighting. Even though wattage was low, and the clear naked bulbs dangled from the tin ceilings, many businessmen favored this medium. No hissing, stinking jets. No danger from leaking fumes. There was encouragement from most quarters, even though few understood how the power worked. When the subject was addressed by the City Council there arose a debate. The Daily Boomerang reported seriously that the Council had decided against building an electric-power plant. And somehow in the debate the ever-present question of the "town-girls" arose which seemed to be centered between accepting the light plant or the girls. The Boomerang's tongue-in-cheek report stated that the Council had decided "the girls must stay. Therefore the electric light must go."

This was a sobering thought and raised quite a hubbub. A few days later the Boomerang printed the Council's second thoughts:

> After public comment was heard and the Council took time to reconsider, their previous decision was over- ruled. The city will be electrically lighted and there will be issued a broad hint to the girls to git.

But that would never do! Such drastic measures were unthinkable. The officials would never be re-elected to office, there would be no cure for the love-sickness, and the city would lose much revenue. After much pro-and-con-ing it was decided the ladies of the night should stay, and the city would get its electricity, too.

Water still ran in the street ditches. Privies still adorned most backyards, but there was running water in many homes now, and with electric or gas lighting available, these innovations became major selling points in any building as was the added flourish of bathtub or indoor toilet, in those few places which could boast.

The condition of Laramie's streets was always a problem. Much of the public headache was caused by overflow from the ditches edging the streets, and from livestock which still roamed freely and illegally about town.

Every spring when the ground thawed, frost rose to the surface and springs bubbled up in yards and streets alike. Boards at street crossings failed of their intended service by being pressed into the muck by wheeled traffic and there was no such thing as mud-free foot passage.

In summer, streets were dusty and had to be watered down daily, occasionally creating unwanted mud puddles where pigs wallowed. Winter streets were snow covered, and became by turns snow- or ice-packed and rutted under traffic. When the snow melted then there was slop and sucking mud. Horse traffic could be followed by the thuck-a-thuck of clinging mud releasing his hooves. Man's passage could be followed by his eloquent cursing. One of the biggest arguments arose over the "disgraceful condition of South C." The decision was made to open the street across the railroad since it was the natural and direct route from the west side to the Eastside School house, as well as for all travel into town from the west-side plains. Thus, the choice location of the Holliday, Bannon-Mandell, and Trabing stores was immediately rewarding.

With only one bridge spanning the Laramie River all east-west traffic flowed along Garfield, and Second Street was the main north-south thoroughfare. Likewise, the accessibility of Front Street with all its delights was immediately at hand.

This lent importance to other mid-town businesses and livery-stables in particular. With travel limited to horseback or buggy and wagon, there was need for many livery barns.

Since Trabing had effectively kept Knadler and Rand from building their big barn next door to the great modern store, the partners were forced to find a different location. They bought John Keane's property on the east side of Third Street at the corner of D (Custer).

The Sentinel reminded its readers that this historic site had "served a vital purpose in the town's early days, for human fruit had hung from the coping of the old log house." This was the place where the infamous trio, Con Wager, Asa Moore and Big Ed Wilson were executed in the fall of 1868.

Knadler and Rand constructed huge double stables which they called the "Windsor" on the Keane property. The newspaper gives dimensions of the building as 132 feet from Third Street to the alley, and opening on the

Custer Street side, with 84 feet the length from north to south. It was forty feet high, giving ample haymow space.

The other main portion of the Windsor was 80 by 82 feet. Next door S. Fuller built another, smaller stable facing onto Third Street. This he called the Thornburgh. Not long after its completion Knadler and Rand sold the Windsor to the three-man partnership of A. L. Haines, W. W. Russell and A. W. Branner. Publicity on the transfer was excessive, and much praise given the social standing and business acumen of the partners. Their knowledge of fine horse-flesh received flattering attention, so did the fact that their business included selling and trading horses. The gentlemen could well have done without so much publicity and praise, for when the three were arrested and hauled into court as horse thieves, it was beyond belief.

The newspaper cried "Haines of all people should know better!" High social rank carries its own obligations.

The three were tried, found guilty and sentenced, Haines and Russell to three years each and Branner to one year.

While in jail awaiting transfer to the Joliet*, Illinois prison, Haines, who had been under a doctor's care for some months, suddenly died. At the coroner's inquest, it was learned that Mrs. Haines took each day's medication to her husband, that she thought he always took each dosage while she was there. The jury decided that death was due to over- medication, whether intentional or accidental was undetermined.

The remaining partners served their terms without apparent incident. Branner evidently did not return to Laramie. Russell did, and opened a second-hand shop

---

* Prisoners were being sent to the Federal Prison at Joliet at that time because it was said to be cheaper per head to board them there than in the Wyoming Penitentiary.

in town. A 1911 City Directory has a picture of W. W. Russell captioned "one of Laramie's old-timers who has made a record."

Two blocks south of the Frontier Hotel on Second Street near Fred Prahl's grocery store, stood Nels Anderson's livery barn which he called the Centennial. The Centennial saloon on Front Street had gone out of business but the Centennial restaurant on South B was still a going concern. The use of the same names for different establishments might indicate some connection, by ownership if nothing else. In this case at least, there was none.

A block north of the Windsor Stables at the corner of Third and C, the old Dayton-Harrison stable had been replaced by a big brick building owned by another Anderson. This barn once provided quarters upstairs for Bill Nye's famous Boomerang news-plant.

Farther north up Third was Ingersoll's Livery, a place popular with ladies of the night for renting driving rigs. Across the intersection stood the red-painted Elkhorn Barn. It was at the Elkhorn that Tom Horn's saddle horse was put up after a long, desperate ride following the shooting of Willie Nickell out in the Laramie Mountains northeast of town. Horn was hanged in 1903 for the crime. (The question of his guilt is still debated.)

With livery barns plentiful and distances removed from restaurants and dining rooms, eating a meal was no longer a contest between diners and flies. On the other hand, if a rider was in need of his steed in a hurry, he might have to resort to alley-ways to reach his mount.

The town was now losing much of its early squalor and assuming the outer skin of gentility. Years earlier, Horace Greeley had remarked that out in the west whenever a cluster of three buildings was raised it was called a city, and that often seemed true. But in 1886 when Laramie had grown and could truthfully lay claim to the "city" tag, it was incorporated and the four-letter word was dropped, thus becoming merely Laramie, a staid and civilized community.

A fine new suburb called West Laramie was laid out about this time across the river west of the penitentiary grounds and lots went on sale. It was apparent from experiments that with water the Wyoming soil could produce bountiful crops. The irrigation canal running on the fringes of the new suburb was sufficient inducement to buyers. This in turn led to another improvement, the construction of a new iron bridge over the Big Laramie River two miles north of the Garfield Street span.

The new bridge was indeed a boon to the city. With the glass works reaching from Canby Street north to Baker on the site of the stockyards, the yards were compelled to move. Their new location on the north edge of town, between the U. P. tracks and river, and bordering the Bath Brewery acres, allowed stock drovers to trail their herds over the new bridge (or swim the river) at that end of town rather than driving the length of the main streets. Businesses also began to move northward and lessened congestion in the old downtown area. It made no difference to Front Street business, however, even with the Drover's Hotel over on North Third Street.

Although some of the earlier businesses had taken bankruptcy, or just left town, there were plenty of going businesses. Stone quarries were still operating and the beautiful peacock stone was being used on some of the new homes in town, and also shipped in quantity out across the nation. Gray stone of fine quality went into the Gothic style Episcopal Church at the corner of Third and North A (now Ivinson Avenue.)

Beautiful cream colored stone from a quarry fifty miles northwest of town was being used more extensively in buildings on the university campus, and the

Cowboy University was beginning to make a name for itself.

Tomato-colored brick was still being made at three different yards on the river's edge. And in the fall plaster mills started working. Only a month later the Laramie Brewery burned, creating a severe, though temporary, drought in town. The facility was soon re-built with business again flourishing at a staggering rate.

A flour mill was erected just north of the electric-light plant, and building was rapidly pushing at the outer edges of town. The City Council found that twenty-six letters of the alphabet were not enough to cover the streets. In 1888 while Dr. Finfrock was Mayor, the Council debated the subject. W. E. Chaplin, editor of the Republican newspaper, and Alderman of the Third Ward, suggested naming a street for the first citizen to settle on it. This caused another debate as to just which person was the first.

In the columns of the Sentinel Hayford grumped about the name change, suggesting that people would get lost and spend the rest of their lives trying to find their way home. He was at his sarcastic best in suggesting various fruits as street names. His remarks were softened when his own name was proposed for one street as the earliest settler. Many words later the suggestion was made to use names of military men.

Even then there was controversy. Questions were raised as to whether or not a certain general had ever served in the area, or even in the western lands. It was finally decided that honorable service could be rendered in any area of the continent, and the name change was effected in June, 1889. Laramie soon became accustomed to the system. It was at that time that the original Front Street was designated Pine and joined the other tree-names on the West Side. Front Street then was freely used in reference to First.

An exuberant item in the Sentinel for November 13, 1886, had stated that the Union Pacific would "erect a fine and commodious railroad depot here. So far people have been accommodated in a public office of a hotel with crowds and much smoking and jostling, all very bad."

But nothing had happened. Businessmen grew tired of waiting for action by the railroad company and drew up a petition in February, 1889, asking the U. P. authorities to build a depot in Laramie. Every businessman in town signed the petition.

A few months later the Sentinel reported that Sidney Dillon had arrived in town and "stepped off the ground" for a new depot. There the project stood for some time. Tickets continued to be sold from the dirty, smokey, crowded office in the Railroad Hotel.

The Railroad Hotel was rented from a company which owned a string of such accommodations along the U. P. line. Mrs. T. D. Abbott had been one of the more popular managers at Laramie, and many residents in town expressed the hope that the widow would be retained when the new depot was built. But she was transferred to the Railroad Hotel at Evanston farther west on the line.

When a new depot was finally built, it too, offered rooms, apartments, dining rooms and freight rooms as well as a special ticket office. The building was one of the finest between Omaha and the west coast and stood on Front Street at the foot of South A street. It was named the Thornburg Hotel in honor of the Major who had lost his life in 1879 during the Ute Indian uprising at the Meeker Agency in Northern Colorado.

Sixteen

The free-wheeling atmosphere which prevailed during the first thirty years of Laramie's existence brought about a generation of ambitious, self-made men. There was nothing too big for them to tackle.

Even the ranchers out in the valley were ambitious, expanding their holdings, if not by purchase, at least through possession, squatting on land which they cursed the nesters for occupying. Their herds of cattle, sheep and/or horses were constantly being up-graded and their wealth was growing and impressive, at least until the years of the "big die-up" when thousands of head of livestock were lost in the heavy winter storms. Many stockmen went broke. So broke, it was said, they had no shadow of their own. Then more and more ranchers saw the advantages of winter feeding which had been practiced by a few.

But money had been made, and it could be made again. There was big talk in town of building a woolen mill to take advantage of the growing sheep industry. The Board of Trade promoted the mill vigorously, as well as pushing for a street railway, and another railroad system, this one from Laramie to Fort Collins and Platteville, Colorado.

These balloons were soon punctured, however, due to increasingly tight money in the East from where the West borrowed. The heavy losses of livestock had adversely affected the Eastern money market, as well as foreign investments. So the mill and railroad ideas were abandoned. Temporarily.

What was organized, though, was the Laramie Race Track Association, and in 1889 a driving track was laid out. Faint traces of the oval may still be seen south of Spring Creek in the open area east of Barratt Avenue.

Another improvement to the town was the paving of some of the downtown streets. Front Street was not one. This did not affect the operations on that interesting row, however. The habitués still had their rousing moments, but they were either of a milder temper or gossip was confined to smaller, tighter circles. At least there seemed to be fewer headlines.

One item that did land on the front pages of the papers was the alleged doings of a dentist named Martin. He was accused of "taking indecent liberties with a young lady patient."

The town (possibly remembering the tragedy of Bridget) rose in righteous wrath. The man was promptly arrested and cast into the courthouse jail. Public meetings were convened and heated discussions were held.

The Sentinel published its sentiments, much more strongly worded than had appeared in the Bridget affair:

> No one who has any respect for himself or the fair name of our city is going to advocate lynch law or mob violence ... but if he is the disgusting and lecherous scoundrel he (Martin) is reported to be ... this community has no further use for him and he has nothing to complain of and no need to be indignant ...

Whether or not the mention of lynch law provided the necessary bravery, a lynch-minded mob descended on the courthouse.

Someone had rushed to the courthouse and reported the coming of the mob to Sheriff Yund. When the group arrived at the door, they were met by the Sheriff and his deputy flanking the old Kentucky hill-man, Judge Micah Saufley, wearing his usual hip hardware. His proficiency with the two guns was so well known the brave visitors paused.

The Judge informed them sternly that Martin was under his protection and he would stop the first man who took a forward step. The men believed him. There was some second thinking and their dedication to community morals soon evaporated. Without bluster or argument they soon left the scene.

Saufley was much admired in the Territory for being as hard-nosed as any westerner and was praised for defending the man who was his prisoner under the law. There were others, however, who cursed and hated him. No one likes to seem cowardly.

The Judge was not re-appointed to Wyoming and soon returned to Kentucky "for his wife's health."

Political games still occupied the time and energy of Laramie's citizens. The conduct of office-holders was much scrutinized and criticized, but as is the case even in modern times, it depended on who, what and when the conduct was rendered. The sin is practically always excusable if it is done with style.

⁂

The red-light district, that "necessary evil", was still much in evidence. The city officials evidently operated on the premise that "to err is human, to keep from being found out is divine."

While Laramie continued to over-look its excesses, other towns were trying for a bit of refinement. Someone tried to blow up a house of ill fame in Cheyenne, but failed because they had been supplied with damp dynamite.

Casper issued an order that "no lewd woman may appear on the streets of the city." Men, no matter how lewd, were free to come and go.

Pictures of some of the frontier's ladies of the line show them as less than pulchritudinous. This apparently mattered not at all — after all, first things came first.

A new City Council took office in April, 1890, with Hayford's remarks ringing in their ears:

The old council (Trabing's regime) left a clean and neat city and a good financial record . . .

And he suggested they go and do likewise. A. S. Peabody was Mayor that year. The new Council again fixed the liquor license fee at $500 (using the old broom of the previous Council) "without discrimination or classification." To prove their non-partisan attitude the Council refused bottle licenses to Della Briggs and to Monte Grover (who was operating at The Blonde's old stand on Grand Avenue, and not yet dead of fear and starvation.)

The Big Horseshoe still swung above Nick Theis' blacksmith shop next door at the corner of Third and Grand. The noise of hammering, the coal-fire smoke from the forge and shouting of men surely provided a less than romantic background for the Grover retiring rooms. Even the thick row of trees planted by Grover between the smithy and brothel could not drown the racket nor dispel the smoke. It probably took more than that to distract from the pleasures of that famous parlor.

The "Institute" on Grand, whatever back-room establishments still operating further south on Third and Fourth Streets, plus those of "known reputation" on First Street, then, presented the same problems to the new Council that had faced all previous officials.

But new problems arose: gamblers tried to force the authorities to license their games. The Territory was to become a state in July, 1890 and the high-rollers were fearful that licensing would not be granted after that since anti-gambling sentiment was so strong. Authorities heard on all sides: "Stop the gambling!"

"One Cheyenne gambler brags he has taken $18.000 out of Laramie in the past few months," the Sentinel roared. "Businesses cry out they are loaded with bad debts on their books, their employees are demoralized and legitimate money diverted to the games ... good, wholesome, restraining laws (should be) enacted against selling liquor to minors and habitual drunks (and) require the keeping of civil, quiet and orderly houses and closings on Sundays. Then enforce same, and any violation (should) require forfeit of license." No comment on the number of times this ordinance had been on the city books or how loosely it had been applied.

In a later issue of his paper Hayford added:

> The parents of Laramie have got to make a desperate effort to save their boys. There are a lot of hell holes and robbers roosts here under the name of Cigar Stores and Billiard Halls which are making every effort to ruin them. This means a great deal more than we choose to tell just now.

The last enigmatic remark was a bit unusual, but Hayford said on different occasions that he was growing old and tired and that might explain his not making a bigger issue of it.

The law passed by the Territorial Legislature in 1888 stated that saloons were to close on Sundays, but as usual enforcement was lax. The City Council of Laramie did succeed in forcing all saloons to move from side streets so that part of the sinning was confined to First Street. Other places were still operating on the fringes of town or out beyond the city limits, wide-open, unrestricted.

Limiting such public houses to First Street seemed to be a good idea. There were even times when the town was quiet enough that other noises could be heard.

Complaints were now being made of the racket and barbarism of "shivarees," and of cowboys racing their horses around the streets at any time of day, yelling and scattering pedestrians like so many chickens.

Then the convicts "revolted" in the penitentiary across the river and attacked Warden Briggs as he herded them from the shops back to their cells. Six felons worked the officer over with his own cane.

Deputies George Stewart and Jerry Marsh began firing at the convicts who were identified as Charles

Archer, Tom Madden, William McGuire, Joe Walker, Kinch McKinney and Conway. Archer was shot in the leg and Madden in the right side, a serious wound, but Dr. Finfrock reluctantly stated that he would live. Three shots were fired at McKinney. All missed.

Disgruntled over the Sunday closings and the enforcement that had been thrust upon the town, the Council in 1892 tried to sneak through an ordinance "opening up the town." The evil deed was done while Mayor N. F. Spicer was out of town, but when he returned he immediately vetoed the measure, having been reminded of the platform on which he was elected. He was hung in effigy on Front Street for his pains (as mentioned earlier).

By then the Laramie Boomerang had changed hands, owners and politics.

The Weekly Sentinel related that "Charlie Rauner is now the ostensible proprietor, 'though it is understood that his democrat pals have put up the dollars and will control the policy of the paper ... We congratulate McKee and Chaplin and the Republican party on having gotten rid of it and (extend) our sympathy to our friend, the enemy."

In 1892, also, Owen Wister had stirred the nation's interest and curiosity about Wyoming and the West with his novel "The Virginian", and added more color to an already colorful vocabulary with the expression "son of a bitch."

"It has always been a favorite expression," a friend wrote to Wister. "But Wyoming is in the son-of-a-bitch stage of . . . civilization and couldn't get along without it."

Many resented the insult to mothers but it became cemented into the language and is now uttered without thought or harmful intent.

At this time, too, a number of the more affluent citizens of Laramie were building new houses. All rather fine houses of that era were hailed as mansions.

Some could be described fairly as being elegant. Among those given particular attention was that which Banker "Evergreen" Ivinson built on his block of land across from the County Courthouse.

Its fine lines and handsome surroundings led to the remark, late in the summer after the place was several months old, that it would make a fine governor's mansion. Someone else took up the theme. Hayford agreed editorially stating that "it was a good idea since Ivinson was about the only man around with enough money to carry on an effective campaign."

That set the political ball rolling. Ivinson was nominated. His slate was unbeatable proclaimed the tub-thumpers.

The entire slate lost.

Ivinson graciously entertained the new governor in the handsome mansion on Thornburg Avenue. (The street now bears the Ivinson name and the mansion houses the Laramie Plains Museum.)

By then, efforts to build the street railway had been revived and had gone beyond the talking stage. The Board of Trade brought the Messrs. McHale and Griffith from Denver to "make the necessary arrangements. The initial point of the road will be the Thornburgh Hotel," the news item stated. (By then Thornburg had acquired an "h") The "initial point" also stalled and died there.

Although Hayford complained of growing old and tired, he was clearly not too tired to make use of his barrage of metaphors in the political arena. Ivinson's loss didn't affect him or his opinions. He wasn't always fond of the banker anyway, for Ivinson was adept with words, too, and they had often crossed swords in debate.

Now the editor of the Sentinel began beating a new drum for city mayor and reminded the public that for the last three years the Republican Mayor of Laramie had been hampered by a Democrat council and police.

"He has been accorded nothing but contempt and (given) no authority," he fumed.

But no one wanted to file for office, and after much fulmination by the Sentinel and party members, John G. Brockway reluctantly agreed to be a candidate. He lost.

People, it seemed, preferred the loose enforcement of city ordinances and the attendant problems created by it.

The new Council appointed George Berner as President, C. W. Bramel became City Attorney, W. N. Roth was Fire Chief with John Williams as Assistant. James Stirling was day policeman and Mames (James?) Moriarty night policeman with Julius Schwatke as night watchman.

"Same old gang," sniffed Hayford.

Warden Briggs resigned from his job at the Pen and was replaced by George Yund and for the next year the city operated in the same old rut.

The fact that C. W. Bramel was now hitting the trail with his temperance lecture "Trials and Triumphs," seemed to amuse Hayford. Without doubt he lost few opportunities to remind the dried-out Bramel of his feud with the Reverend Brother Edmondson. Hayford twitted the "Democrat organ," the Boomerang, for "pitching into Councilman Lohlein for voting against the gambling ordinance. But," the Sentinel pointed out, "they seem to think it all right for Councilman (James) Vine, a Democrat, to vote the same way. The Council has passed an ordinance prohibiting gambling in any form. (But) some thought it should not prohibit shaking dice for cigars."

From the early squalor of tent-and-shack-town clinging grimly to the grassy river banks in 1868, Laramie had now achieved "city" status with a fine university and a stable economy backed by the Union Pacific Railroad and increased ranching out in the great Laramie Basin. Even the catastrophic depression of 1893 - '97 couldn't hold it down. Indeed Hayford expressed the opinion, as did others, that the economic problems were a good thing.

> For one good result will grow out of it. The present generation, which got its reckless habits and extravagant tastes in the days of our great war when dollars were so plentiful and cheap, will be taught lessons of industry, thrift and economy which have been forgotten and discarded since the days of our fathers . . .

Tight money always has the same effect. People are drawn closer together and are more considerate and sensitive to others' needs. Misfortune seems to breed compassion.

Even celebrations were different, exuberant as always, but less lavish than in other years. The Christmas holidays passed off pleasantly and peacefully. Unusually gay parties were held with more social gatherings than were "ever known of." And "Not even one drunk!"

But New Years was a different matter. Some celebrants continued greeting the new year for several days. Among that group were Tom Watkins and Tom Price who had taken their celebration too long and heartily and got into a brawl which ended when Watkins bit off a piece of the Price lip. Watkins was sent to prison for a year. He got no time off for good behavior as had Ritter, the County Treasurer of earlier time. Maybe he should have stolen public funds instead of drinking.

In March, 1895, came the disastrous fire which destroyed the Trabing Company's imposing store and brought about the collapse of its merchandising empire. The newspapers remarked that the town was "swarming with insurance men" for weeks.

Trabing's, of course, continued in business in other quarters on a drastically reduced scale and never recovered from that disaster. The death of young George Cordiner beneath a falling brick wall no doubt haunted the portly August Trabing to the end of his days.

The fire greatly altered the flow of business on the

town's front streets. Other groceries and markets now drew trade, and hitching rails on other streets now stood full.

In April, 1895, Judge J. H. Hayford "old and full of years," put aside his famous teaspoon and retired from the newspaper business. In the April 17th issue of the Sentinel he announced:

> With the present volume the Sentinel completes the 26th volume and we have decided to suspend publication . . . this seems to be as good a time to bid goodby to our readers (as any). . . . 'Laramie will be well represented by the papers remaining . . .'

There were four in publication in town at that time.

The last issue which appears in the 1893 - '95 book of the Sentinel bears the names of Huntington and Gillette as proprietors and publishers and bears the date May 25, 1895.

So the books were closed on the Sentinel, that bold Voice of the Plains, and the opinionated, irascible much-admired Hayford went on to other things.

He sold life insurance and served as Police Judge and Justice of the Peace for his beloved Gem City, and as Judge of the Second Judicial District of the State of Wyoming.

The Casper Derrick congratulated him for his "impartial manner on the bench." He was "commended as eminently qualified to grace the position (of Judge) ... and exhibited a profound knowledge of the law and (exercised) common sense in the disposition of every case."

In exchanging his editorial pen for the judge's gavel Hayford again demonstrated his talents and ability to live a full life and chew tobacco at the same time. He died in 1902.

Seventeen

The big waves so often created on the Laramie news scene did not die with the demise of the Sentinel. The Laramie Republican and the Boomerang kept up a lively feud until they merged some years later. The Republican liked to brag on being first with the news while the Boomerang boasted of being "always accurate." Neither always fulfilled their boasts.

There were fewer references to the shady side of town, now, but opportunities were still available for learning the art of dissipation from specialists.

Along with the temper of the fading century the town changed, too. Several of the businesses which had furnished a living for so many in Laramie cut back their operations, others ceased altogether and new ones came in. Ranching and dry-landfarming in the area lured prospective settlers. This affected the population in a modest way. Laramie grew from 6,388 in 1890 to a nice round 8,200 in 1900.

Ranching remained one of the industries that continued to flourish despite many set-backs, and came to occupy the public mind and imagination. The cowboy image painted by Owen Wister and Ned Buntline fostered the public's longing for heroes, and the "romance of the range" lived for decades.

Not all the range-heroes fit the "clean-living wholesome" image the stories projected, for when the cowboys hit town after the prolonged drought of range riding, many were just as rowdy, boisterous and noisome and prone to seek the pleasures of Front Street as had their predecessors of tiehack and railroad building days. It was reported that of the 174 convicts in the

Penitentiary, 24 of them were cowboys, and there was one sheepherder.

Nor was all cowboying done out on the range, even in later days. One "mad bull" invaded a yard in West Laramie keeping the family indoors and pawing dirt and bellowing his frustrations. Police were called and with their usual tact finally persuaded the "critter" to return to his own pen. The owner was ordered to rebuild his fences.

Not so docile was another "John Doe Bull" which became separated from his companions and paraded his bovine majesty around Grand Avenue where the action once centered in the old Tivoli, the Brooklyn Shades or at Murphy's Bar and Diana's corner. The "gentleman cow" was finally captured by a bevy of mainstreet cowboys after several hours' chase.

The cowboy image was given greater exposure when numerous "bucking bronco" exhibitions were held. Bronc riding was not new, but as public performances they were. Riders frequently bet on their ability to stay aboard their bronc and keep a silver dollar in each stirrup beneath their boots. Most often they won, too.

Lander is credited with holding the first commercial rodeo in Wyoming in 1893. Two years later the Laramie Fair Association held its first public exhibition at the city stockyards at the end of a Labor Day celebration. Other such shows by the "Laramie Riders" were given before an excited, admiring public and a new form of hero worship began. "Laramie" became almost synonymous with "cowboy." The new football team organized by the University was given the title of "Cowboys."

Mingled now with the regular noises of the town, the still-busy railroad and its shops and a growing passion for the "romantic range-life" that never really existed, were the different, but just as pungent, smells and sounds of the horseless carriage.

The first gasoline-buggy built in Wyoming was constructed by Elmer Lovejoy in 1897 - '98 in his machine shop on South Second Street across from the site of the old Frontier Hotel lots. Lovejoy's machine was guaranteed to cover more miles in less time than any horse could. It also relieved the wagon-weary traveler of sitting on a hard seat watching the swaying rumps of the horses and comparing them with those of various acquaintances.

The automobile seemed a fitting way to end the old century and usher in the new twentieth. It signaled the end of a slower-paced, more gracious mode of living where ladies poured tea with delicate wrist and sweet housewifely attention, and men gathered around their card tables with their gossip. It introduced a noisier, faster, far less majestic style of life, and Laramie greeted the New Year's arrival eagerly, noisily, strutting and bold, but still bawdy and confident. The town joined the rest of the world in celebrating, toasting the new century in expectation of a splendid prosperity and the sweet excitement of future.

Many of the tales warmed by the Forty Liars are now told: of happenings over thousands of miles of the far land, of the wide, waiting plains, its dips and rises, its dark, silent, hidden canyons and rugged ridges lifting to the shining, sublime mountains. A vital time of wanderings, of conquering a wilderness, uniting two vast oceans and building a great nation; tales of the coursing buffalo hunts, of miners and trappers, the subduing of a wild, free people; tales of brawling, lusty men and women, of those caught in their erotic servility, and the stories of every frontier town and their Front Streets.

The fires have dimmed. But the West has left its bright wish on multitudes and the magic still lives.

End

Maps

These maps were drawn from information in the land records of the Albany County Clerk's Office, Laramie.

Index of Names